I PROMISE YOU

I Promise You

God's Words of Love
and Encouragement

LYNN BROOKSIDE

Servant Publications
Ann Arbor, Michigan

Vine Books is an imprint of Servant Publications especially designed to serve evangelical Christians.

All scripture quotations are from the NEW INTERNATIONAL VERSION unless otherwise marked. © 1973, 1978, 1984 by International Bible Society. Used by permission of Zondervan Publishing House. All rights reserved. Scripture quotations marked TLB are taken from *The Living Bible*. © 1971 by Tyndale House Publishers, Wheaton, Illinois. Scripture quotations marked NKJV are taken from the NEW GENEVA STUDY BIBLE (New King James Version). © 1995 by Foundation for Reformation. Scripture quotations marked RSV are taken from the REVISED STANDARD VERSION. © 1972 by Thomas Nelson, Inc., New York. Scripture quotations marked NASB are taken from the NEW AMERICAN STANDARD BIBLE. © 1977 by The Lockman Foundation, A Corporation Not for Profit, La Habra, California.

Published by Servant Publications
P.O. Box 8617
Ann Arbor, Michigan 48107

Cover design: Diane Bareis
Cover photograph: Dennis Frates

96 97 98 99 00 10 9 8 7 6 5 4 3 2 1

Printed in the United States of America
ISBN 0-89283-928-7

Library of Congress Cataloging-in-Publication Data

Brookside, Lynn.
    I promise you : God's words of love and encouragement / Lynn Brookside.
        p.   cm.
    Includes indexes.
    ISBN 0-89283-928-7
    1. Trust in God—Meditations. 2. God—Love—Meditations.   3. Devotional calendars.   I. Title.
BV4811.B745   1996
242—dc20   96-2172
                                                                              CIP

Dedication

To Daniel and Angela

who make being a mom such a delight.

Contents

Acknowledgements

John Donne's statement, "No man is an island," holds particularly true for writers, I think. It would be impossible for me to list all of the people who have helped and inspired me in so many, many ways. There are a few, however, who deserve special mention.

First, I want to thank all the wonderful people at Servant Publications who not only care for every element of book production but for me as well. Words are too feeble to express my thanks.

I owe a particular debt of gratitude to my former pastor, Dr. Richard P. Kaufmann, who is now pastoring at Redeemer Presbyterian Church (PCA) in Manhattan. You're responsible for planting the seeds of a great many of my "Ah hah!" experiences with the Lord over the past few years—experiences that have taught me many of the truths I share here. Your wisdom, patience, and trustworthiness, along with the fact that you are so completely yielded to the Lord, make you an awesome man. Thanks also to you, Liz, for your friendship to me and constant support for Dick, as well as your own quiet example of godly womanhood. I miss you both immensely, but keep your fork....

Thanks also to our new pastor at New Life Church, Rev. Daniel E. Deaton, his wife Barbara, and their daughters, Katie, Sarah, and Emily. I'm grateful that God has knit our hearts together. It was worth the wait! I look forward to many years of friendship and rich partnership in ministry.

And thanks to Jane Johnson and Laurie Mallon. Both of you helped me immeasurably with this book by being my theological "safety net," faithfully pointing out to me those instances when a theological premise was sloppy or misleading so that I could be a "workman who... correctly handles the word of truth."

Of all those I asked to suggest Scripture promises, Nancy Benson wins the prize, hands down. Nancy, the consistency of your thoughtfulness boggles my mind. Thank you.

And an extra special thank you to Don and Donna Bandow. You have not only "parented" me, but you have so often and fervently upheld me in prayer that there are no words meaningful enough to describe the ways you have enriched my life.

And to Emily Boronkay, her husband Danny, and children Josh and Bekkah. Em, you have a special gift for pointing out that distant spot of light when the storm seems to howl around me.

And Cathy Mitchell. Few people could nurture my heart the way you do while keeping me on my toes by constantly challenging my beliefs. Thanks, also, to your sweet husband, Keith, who keeps me laughing, as well as Graham and Bailey.

Also Dr. Peter and Rebecca Jones and family. How can I possibly thank you enough? You are the embodiment of Philemon 7.

And thanks to my friends, Knox and Marilyn DeLise, Dr. and Mrs. Ed Clowney, Dr. and Mrs. Mark Futato, Peggy Merrill, and so many, many others. Each of you has added to my life in ways too numerous to mention here.

In addition, God has blessed me with a spiritual mother who wrote the book on *Spiritual Mothering*, Susan Hunt. Thank you for taking me into your heart and your busy life and for being such a wonderful model of godly womanhood. And thank you for your faithful friendship and prayers, for caring so deeply and calling me so consistently to a stronger and better faith in our Lord. My heart is full of joy and gratitude each time I think of you.

Thank you to my spiritual daughters as well. You know who you are. You are my joy and crown and I love you dearly.

And to my entire family at New Life Presbyterian Church in Escondido, especially Cecilia Andis, JoAnn Wilson, and all my precious sisters and fellow members of the WIC Council, past and present. Thanks for your input, your encouragement, your understanding, your loving acceptance, and especially your prayers.

Finally, my loving thanks to my dear brother Gerard Merrill, who is finally free from pain. I weep for myself and all those you left behind but I rejoice for you. What a wondrous homecoming it must have been. Enjoy yourself, my dear brother, and hold a place near you at the table for me. It is with great joy that I anticipate the day I will be free to join you there.

Truly, the best is yet to come.

Introduction

During my prayer time one day, approximately eleven years ago, I was suddenly overcome with a flash of Holy Spirit-inspired clarity. In a single instant of searing honesty I came face-to-face with the realization that my commitment to God was puny and halfhearted and that fear was the true god of my life. In that moment I was overcome by grief and genuine guilt. It was in that instant that my life was changed forever because, frightened though I was, I knew that I could never again settle for anything less than an absolute commitment to God's purpose for my life. Looking back now I can see that the force of my decision was comparable to a bomb exploding, although I was too close to my struggle at the time to have more than a vague impression of an extraordinarily painful and—in the beginning—agonizingly slow reordering of my life.

From my vantage point at this moment, however, I can see that my life now stands so significantly altered as to be nearly unrecognizable, yet, strangely, there is also a quality of familiarity. You see, I always had what I now realize was a Holy Spirit-inspired understanding of the way my life should be. From childhood I had dreamed of it, longed for it. Only my fear—which is merely another way of saying my lack of trust in God—held me back. I cannot now view my current life without feeling a sense of "Ah, yes. *This* is the way I knew it should be." Although I must hasten to add, along with Paul, that "I do not consider myself yet to have taken hold of it. But one thing I do: Forgetting what is behind and straining toward what is ahead, I press on toward the goal to win the prize for which God has called me..." (Phil 3:13,14).

For the majority of those eleven years I struggled more or less alone. I was not personally acquainted with Christians who wanted or understood how to claim more than a lukewarm Christian existence. In many ways my journey has been considerably easier these past four-and-a-half years, since I have begun to fellowship with a local body of believers in which the majority also endeavor, to the best of their ability, to place God before self. In other ways my journey has been harder because their example and encouragement was wedded to a far greater accountability than I had ever known before. But the "marriage" has been so beneficial, I have absolutely no complaints.

In these eleven years I have faced countless things I never previously knew lay within my heart and mind. Many times my spiritual muscles have protested the stretching they were forced to endure. Often I faltered—again, out of fear—and might not have found the courage or strength to carry on had it not been for members of my church who came alongside, encouraging, correcting, and always, always praying. God especially blessed me for three-and-a-half of those four-and-a-half years with a pastor and friend, Dick Kaufmann, who weekly accomplished the feat of simultaneously massaging the balm of God's Word into my aching spiritual muscles while inspiring an ever-increasing determination within me to reach for more, to stretch farther and still farther. It has been a grueling and—occasionally—frightening time, and the most exciting, joyous time I have ever known.

Yes, I did say "frightening." There are some who would prefer me to say that my fears were immediately relieved the moment I chose to turn from my former life and seek "the prize" wholeheartedly. They were not. Throughout many of those eleven years I had countless sleepless nights, nights replete with trembling hands and pounding heart, nights when I walked the floor rather than risk the darkness and the nightmares that I knew would inevitably storm the gateway of my sleep. There were other times when fear cut through me suddenly, snatching my breath away like an icy wind. But our God is a mighty God, faithful and true. He walked with me. He soothed nerves afire with pain and overwhelming sorrow. And he was my patient teacher. You see, I would have learned nothing if God had swept my fears away with a mighty stroke of his hand. The lessons I learned as I faced my fears could produce the fruit of righteousness and peace only if I walked *through* them, one tentative step at a time.

When I began my journey, I only vaguely understood that the Bible contained the answers I needed and, try as I might, I was unable to comprehend how the Scriptures applied to the day-to-day events of my life. Slowly, God taught me biblical ways to cope with grief and depression, anger, worry... and fear. I learned to run to God with my pain, to rest in his arms where no monsters of the night could reach me. And I learned to measure myself and my struggles against the standard of the Scriptures. In short, I learned to *trust* God. Suddenly, obedience no longer seemed like "too much to ask" because it was so utterly founded in trust.

I am an entirely different person now. I know who I am in Jesus Christ and I know that the purpose for my life—for all of life—is to glorify God. What great confidence that knowledge instills in me! I've come to know the truth and it has set me free.

Another lesson I learned along the way was one of balance. Once I had learned the sweetness of obedience I found myself concentrating wholly on the areas of my life where I still fell short, omitting almost entirely the refreshment available to me in God's promises. While it is true that I must not casually dismiss a single one of my God-given responsibilities, it is equally important for me to be perpetually conscious of God's promises. To lose this awareness puts me at risk of growing weary in well-doing.

This book is an exploration of those promises, designed to provide spiritual food for people with various needs, at varying stages of life. For those who are hurting and in need of comfort and assurance, the devotions may be read alone. Those seeking an in-depth Bible study will want to contemplate the Scripture references at the end of each devotion. In any case, the devotions are not necessarily meant to be read in order. If one doesn't seem to apply to your present circumstances, look for one that is more suitable.

It has been a joy and privilege to write this book. God's promises continually infuse my spirit with awe. There have been many times in its writing when the magnitude of one of God's promises has forced me to momentarily suspend my work because I was unable to see through tears of gratitude, unable to think because I was awash in a renewed consciousness of the intensity and purity of

God's love. It is my hope that you, too, will find in the promises contained here, tears of joy and a new awareness of God's love... and that these things will bring about an ever-increasing trust in our Lord and Savior, Jesus Christ.

Some will be surprised by the fact that this book is written in the first person, as if God were the speaker. I, too, was surprised when my editor asked me to write in the first person. Let me assure you that there was never a single day when I took the assignment lightly. It was a task I approached with abundant prayer and with reverent fear and trembling. Yet, I must admit, I now realize that here really is no better way to write such a book. Writing about God's promises tends to place the attention on the writer rather than our faithful God who accomplishes all He has promised.

Lynn Brookside
Escondido, California

PART ONE

God's Promise of Love

1 ✋ My Promises to You

*His divine power has given us everything we need for life
and godliness through our knowledge of him who called us
by his own glory and goodness. Through these he has given
us his very great and precious promises....*

2 Peter 1:3-4

Dance among my promises, my grace-full child.
Twirl them around your heart and practice them in your mind.
Make them your own.
Pronounce each syllable often and quietly until each one is
    sealed within your spirit.
Ponder them until the very air you breathe is scented with them.
Because, you see, dwelling on my promises can be the prelude to
    their fulfillment.

Close your eyes to circumstances. Consider, instead, the character of the One who has promised. Eyes can fail you, perspective can trick you, but my promises are sure for all time.[1]

Do not look down at the greatness of your need or you may stumble and fall. Look up, at me. Turn your eyes to behold my enduring, faithful Word.[2] I am not a man; I cannot lie. My will for you never wavers.[3]

The promises you read in my Word were not written capriciously, according to the writer's whim. They were written at my directive through men inspired by my Holy Spirit.[4]

My Word is infused with all my power. When I speak, my words become substance. When I command, all of creation must obey.[5]

My words are more powerful than all you can touch, taste, and see. All those things shall one day cease to be. But my Word remains true forever.[6]

Just as surely as the rain that falls on the mountains and flows to the valleys makes the farmer's crops green and fruitful, my Word flows from my mouth and accomplishes all I have commanded.[7]

[1] Peter 1:23; [2] Psalms 33:4; 119:89-90; [3] Numbers 23:19; [4] 2 Peter 1:20-21; [5] Psalm 33:6-11; [6] Mark 13:31; [7] Isaiah 55:10-11

2 ∽ When You Doubt My Promises

*Praise be to the Lord, the God of Israel, who with his hands
has fulfilled what he promised with his mouth to my father
David.*

2 Chronicles 6:2

I am your ever-faithful Father-God. I do not change like shifting
shadows; I will fulfill with my hands all I have promised you
through my Holy Scriptures.
I know how easy
   —almost automatic—
   it is for you to dismiss some of my promises
   as having been meant for someone
   more "deserving."
But what father does not want his children to believe that he means
   it when he offers them something they need?[1]
I am faithful.
It is impossible for me to break my promises to you.
It would violate my very nature.
I have pledged to keep my covenant of love to a thousand genera-
   tions of those who love me
   and keep my commandments.[2]
And I have the power to do what I have promised.[3]
Your Enemy will make you doubt me if he can. He often whispers
   doubts in your ears. You're afraid he may be right.
He is a liar and the father of lies![4]
You need not fear him *or* his lies.
I have given you the courage to call him by his true name. I have
   purchased for you the freedom to name him as a liar. He will
   skulk away when you confront him with the truth,
I promise you.
Here is the truth!
When you claim my promises for yourself
   you are not being selfish or greedy.

You are being an obedient child
    and it will be credited to you as righteousness.[5]

[1]James 1:16; Luke 11:11-13; [2]Deuteronomy 7:9; [3]Romans 4:20-21; [4]John 8:44; [5]James 2:23

3 ✥ I Tend You Like a Father

*As a father has compassion on his children, so the Lord has
compassion on those who fear him; for he knows how we
are formed, he remembers that we are dust.... But from
ever-lasting to everlasting the Lord's love is with those who
fear him, and his righteousness with their children's children—with those who keep his covenant and remember to
obey his precepts.*

Psalm 103:13-18

I tend you gently,
  like a Father,
  even in your impatience to get on with things.
You strive so, straining to blossom fully and quickly,
  afraid life's desert wind will wither your flower
  and blow it away,
  so that even the earth where you were planted
  forgets you were ever there.[1]
You stamp your feet when things do not happen
  quickly enough,
  boldly enough ...
  abundantly enough.
And I remember that you are dust
  and show you my compassion anyway.[2]

I pour out my compassion on all those who are afraid to venture
from my side—those who understand the danger that exists outside
of my protective embrace—and on their children as well. If, when
you hear my Word, you listen and take it seriously; if you acknowledge my power and strive to remember my Word through the diligent practice of it; then my compassion is for you and for your children, no matter who you are or what you do or how far you have
yet to go in your walk with me.

Trust me.

When desert winds blow through your life,
  trust me to eventually lead you beside still waters.
Trust that my goodness and mercy are woven
  even into the elements of your life
  with which you are most frustrated.
Trust that
  —even as you walk through the valley of the shadow of death—
I mean you only good, never harm.[3]
Claim my peace. Call upon me to make your heart sing songs of
  hope and trust even in the midst of the storm.
I will do it.

[1]Psalms 103:15-16; [2]Psalms 103:13-14; [3]Psalms 23

4 ❧ Passport to God's Kingdom

*For he has rescued us out of the darkness and gloom of
Satan's kingdom and brought us into the Kingdom of his
dear Son.*

Colossians 1:13, TLB

You were once dominated by darkness;
   evil held you in its sway and
         there was no escape.[1]
Now you live in hope
   … no longer cowering fearfully in the dark.[2]
Your citizenship has been transferred
   to the Kingdom of light
where my dearly beloved son, Christ Jesus, lives and rules.[3]
   Do not fear the unseen forces of darkness.
Hold to your hope as an anchor amid the storms of life
   so that you will not be tossed by each passing wind.[4]
You can put your faith in my promises because I am faithful.[5]
   The forces of darkness are not all-powerful,
       ever-present, or all-knowing.
         They are defeated.
You are no longer guilty but forgiven.…
   You are mine,
      no longer a slave
        but free![6]
           Free to serve your rightful King.

Let your freedom inspire you to perform loving deeds and
encourage others to do the same.[7] You have been liberated without
cost (to you) and you have received a rich deposit of your future
glory. You are secure in the purpose for which I created you. Take
joy in living as a much-loved citizen of my kingdom. Take comfort
in your unconditional job security, doing all the work I created and
equipped you to do; the work I planned for you before you were
born… before time began.[8]

Rejoice! You have the incomparable pleasure of living in love, demonstrating my love to others so that they, too, may one day have their citizenship transferred to the Kingdom of light.

[1]Romans 8:5-7, Ephesians 2:1-3; [2]Colossians 1:27; [3]Philippians 3:20; [4]Hebrews 6:13-20; [5]Hebrews 10:23; [6]Romans 8:1-2; Galatians 4:7; [7]Hebrews 10:24; [8]Ephesians 2:1-10

5 ᴥ Rooted in My Love

*I pray that out of his glorious riches he may strengthen you
with power through his Spirit in your inner being, so that
Christ may dwell in your hearts through faith. And I
pray that you, being rooted and established in love, may
have power, together with all the saints, to grasp how wide
and long and high and deep is the love of Christ, and to
know this love that surpasses knowledge—that you may be
filled to the measure of all the fullness of God.*

Ephesians 3:16-19

Rejoice, my lovely child,
    and open your heart to
    receive the full measure of who I am.
Say "All is well" and mean it,
    because you may approach me with freedom and confidence
    regardless of your circumstances.[1]
I am able to do more,
    both *for* you and *in* you,
    than you have ever dreamed in your wildest flight of fancy.[2]
So receive all I have for you with open arms.
Even your troubles are meant to sink the roots of your heart
    down deep into the rich soil of my love.
    I have filled you with my glory.
I allow troubles to assail you
    for just a little while
    so you will know that the glory that shines through you
    in the midst of trouble
    is mine.[3]
An understanding of my love is of greater worth
    than all the knowledge you will ever acquire.
It is in union with other believers that you
    will be able to grasp the scope and depth of my love.
It is together with other believers that you have
    access to the power you need

to demonstrate my glory through love.
Join with your family—my family—and claim my promises.
Sink your roots deep, like a tree planted by a stream.[4]
Learn to rest in my unconditional love.

[1] Ephesians 3:12; [2]Ephesians 3:20-21; [3]Ephesians 3:13;
[4]Psalms 1:1-3

6 ℘ Grace to Meet Your Needs

*For we do not have a high priest who is unable to sympa-
thize with our weaknesses, but we have one who has been
tempted in every way, just as we are—yet was without sin.
Let us then approach the throne of grace with confidence,
so that we may receive mercy and find grace to help us in
our time of need.*

Hebrews 4:15-16

You think I have not noticed that your back is to the wall,
   don't you?
You think I don't know how you feel;
   that I cannot possibly sympathize with you
   because you brought your predicament on yourself.
Does a father abandon his child
   simply because she is weak?
Because your brother, Jesus, suffered when he was tempted,
   he knows how to help you when you face temptations.[1]
He remembers what it is like to wrestle with weakness.[2]
In him you may approach me with freedom and confidence.[3]
I never grow tired of showing you my compassion. I will be faithful
   to the end of all eternity.[4]
I watch over you as a loving Father, never sleeping.[5]
Even when you do not know what to pray for
   and cannot even imagine how to begin finding your way,
I will be faithful to pour out my grace upon you.
I always know what you need, even when you don't.[6]
Ask me to meet your need. Seek my wisdom.
Approach me with confidence.
When you ask
   I will give.
      When you seek
         I will see that you find.
            When you knock
               I will open.[7]

I am the maker of heaven and earth. My grace is available to you at all times, simply ask.[8]

[1]Hebrews 2:18; [2]Matthew 26:41; [3]Ephesians 3:12; [4]Lamentations 3:22-23; [5]Psalms 121:4; [6]Romans 8:26-27; [7]Matthew 7:7; [8]Psalms 124:8

7 ❧ Returning to Faith

*I have been crucified with Christ; it is no longer I who
live, but Christ lives in me; and the life which I now live
in the flesh I live by faith in the Son of God, who loved me
and gave himself for me.*

Galatians 2:20, NKJV

Your arid soul burns within you.
Your sun-bleached bones feel
   as if they will shatter and break.
You look for relief within and find none
   ... only a boundless sea of searing sand.
You have been away from me too long, my precious one.
Not a single tree or blade of grass is visible
   from where you stand.
But wait.
Come, enjoy the view from where I am.
Come see the lovely foliage,
   smell the fragrant lily blossoms
   growing at the foot of the cross.
You were crucified with Christ, remember.
That truth supplants all others,
   even when you temporarily choose to wander
   from the source of refreshing for your soul.[1]
Do you see?
Viewed through my Son,
   your soul doesn't look like a desert;
   it is a flourishing field.
I gave you a new heart and a new spirit
   when you believed in Christ's name.[2]
His victory makes all things new.
And my gifts, given for my Son's sake,
   cannot be scorched by the sun;
   they are indestructible.[3]

Hurry now! Enter my presence with a repentant heart so that I may drench your sun-parched soul with rains of forgiveness.[4] Enter without hesitation, because I have longed for your return.[5]
My angels rejoice with me![6]
Welcome!

[1]Psalms 42:1; Proverbs 13:19; [2]Ezekiel 36:26; Ephesians 4:23-24; [3]Colossians 3:1-10; Matthew 6:19-21; [4]Acts 3:19; [5]Luke 15:11-24; [6]Luke 15:10

8 ✒ Feeling Lonely

God sets the lonely in families, he leads forth the prisoners with singing....

Psalm 68:6

Loneliness turns a heart into an empty cavern. It fashions prison bars from the dread of another day spent alone. It steals the spirit... the voice... the laughter... of all who are imprisoned so.

My precious child, I have broken through your prison bars.

I have released the shackles of your loneliness and dread. I have freed you to sing praises to me.[1]

Come out of your prison and claim your inheritance.[2]

I have not left you orphaned... fatherless;

I have placed you in my family

so that you will never be alone again...[3]

never again wander as a stranger

in an unfamiliar land.[4]

Your faith in Christ has sealed your adoption into my eternal family.[5]

When loneliness overtakes you, when you toss on your bed and find no comfort because of the aching of your heart, when your hands tremble with fear and dread,

whisper to your heart to be content,

remind yourself that you are never alone...

I am always with you![6]

I am your comforter, your ever-present help, and I fill you with strength.[7]

Even in your greatest hour of need

I will not leave you.[8]

My strong arms will keep you from falling.

I will drive away your twin enemies,

fear and dread.[9]

I am never far from you. In fact, you live your entire life within the circle of my power and will. I have appointed every breath you take, every muscle's movement... indeed, the very essence of your being. You are my offspring in the strictest sense of the term![10]

I have provided you with a Brother who is more than a brother... a Brother who understands your every need... a Brother who gave his life to secure your adoption into my family. Even at this very moment he stands ready to usher you into my presence.[11]

Come!

[1]Exodus 15:1-13; [2]Matthew 25:31-46; [3]2 Corinthians 6:18; [4]Ephesians 2:19; [5]Galatians 3:26; [6]Matthew 28:20; [7]2 Corinthians 1:3-4; Psalms 46:1; [8]Isaiah 41:10; [9]Deuteronomy 33:27; [10]Acts 17:28; [11]Hebrews 4:15-16

9 ♂ When You Are Afraid of Dying

For he [God] himself has said, "I will never leave you nor forsake you." So we may boldly say: "The Lord is my helper; I will not fear."

Hebrews 13:5-6

You're frightened...
  afraid of being alone...
  afraid of the mysterious future.
But, my precious jewel, if you have trusted in the blood and righteousness of Jesus Christ, *your* future is not a mystery, it is well provided for.[1]

Rest in my provision.
I will not leave you
  —either in life or in Life.

Yes, you begin to see it now, don't you? You were already dead; you passed from death to Life when you believed.[2] Death (as you call it) has no power over you.

Flesh and blood can find no resting place with me. It is necessary to be changed in order to join me in heaven. Death is a way to enter into that changed state. To the believer, death is not death, it is merely a departure. It is a glorious homecoming... a wondrous victory celebration![3]

Turn fear away at the door. Do not allow the mysterious part of death to overshadow that which is certain. No one knows the day and hour that she will be summoned to prepare for her coronation day. But you can be absolutely sure that *I* know the number of your days on earth. I recorded them in ages past. Satisfy yourself with that and look toward your glorious inheritance instead.[4]

Do not fear the grave. The grave has no power over you. You will never inhabit it. I have claimed you for myself, to reign with me forever.[5]

[1]1 Peter 5:1-5, 14; John 6:47, 51; 14:1-4; [2]John 5:24; [3]1 Corinthians 15:50-55; [4]Psalms 37:18; [5]Psalms 49:15

10 ᕻ When You Need Hope

*May the God of hope fill you with all joy and peace as you
trust in him, so that you may overflow with hope by the
power of the Holy Spirit.*

Romans 15:13

Do you trust me, dear one?

Do you believe that I want only what is best for you? You
acknowledge that you are in need of hope. Will you trust me with
your circumstances so that I can fill you with hope?

Hope flows from faith in me and nothing else.

Satan wants to defeat you through your circumstances, but *he* is
already defeated.

So run this race with perseverance.

Fix your faith on the figure at the finish line—my son, Jesus
Christ—who is both the originator and perfecter of your faith.[1]

If you keep your eyes focused on the prize that will be yours
when you reach the finish line, you will be able to endure in hope
just as he did.[2]

Along with hope I will give you joy so that you may rejoice in
me always.

Do not be anxious about anything.
Entrust your circumstances to me in prayer,
    praying thankfully
    both for the trial and for the answer.
Along with hope and joy comes peace.
My peace belongs to all who love my law, and
    nothing can cause them to stumble.[3]
Trust that I have the power to give you peace
    despite your circumstances...
    a peace that cannot be explained with human reason...
    a peace that will stand guard over your heart and mind
    so that Satan cannot steal your hope.[4]

Trust me and you will overflow with hope by the power of my Holy Spirit.

[1]Hebrews 12:1-2; [2]Philippians 3:14; [3]Psalms 119:165; [4]Philippians 4:4-7

11 ✣ I Am Always with You

...You are a forgiving God, gracious and compassionate,
slow to anger and abounding in love.

Nehemiah 9:17b

There is no one who will ever love you
    as I do, my precious child
    ... no one will gently care for you the way I do.
There is no one as immense, as powerful
    ... no one else who has pledged such love that
    the pledge can never be broken.[1]
Trust me now. Your challenges have not escaped my notice.
    I am always watching.
You are perpetually before me.[2]
My eyes never drift indifferently to more serene vistas,
    leaving you on your own...
    alone.[3]
I am always with you—giving you strength,
    even when you don't feel particularly strong.
Choose not to dwell on the way you feel.
Feelings are transitory, shifting like dry sand under your feet.
I am trustworthy.
My Word is dependable.
Place your feet on the Rock of my promises, where even an earth-
    quake has no power over you.
Remain with me and do not give in to fear.
Sink your roots into my Word.[4]
Drink deeply of my Living Water and be refreshed.[6]
I will prove my faithfulness
    again and again
    and again.[7]

[1]Nehemiah 9:32a; [2]Isaiah 49:16; [3]Deuteronomy 31:6; [4]Jeremiah 17:8; 1 John 4:18; [5]John 4:10 [6]Acts 3:19-20; [7]Psalms 36:5-9; Lamentations 3:22-23

12 ⁓ When You Feel Powerless

... When I am weak, then I am strong.
2 Corinthians 12:10

You think of me as an unbending taskmaster looking for a chance
to give you a failing mark. You're afraid that I'll examine you
and find you lacking. Not so, my child.
You are precious to me!
I know you don't *feel* precious when you are weak.
You regard your weakness as
repulsive,
even frightening.
That's not the way I see it. I regard your weakness as an opportunity to make my grace thrive in you[1]—a chance to help you
shine in my reflected glory.[2]
Don't you see?
Your weakness is cause for celebration![3]
If you were not weak you would never have a chance to
demonstrate the magnitude of my grace.
You would never have the opportunity to
fathom the depth of my love.
You would have no reason to
praise me for delivering you from your difficulty.

Rejoice in the opportunity to illustrate *my* all-surpassing power.
When your weakness causes you to draw on my strength, you
demonstrate my goodness by showing others that you can't be
crushed even when you're pressed on every side. You confirm that,
in me, it is possible to be perplexed without despairing. You provide
living evidence that persecution does not mean that I have abandoned you.[4]
Glory in the chance to be a walking, breathing testimony to my
everlasting goodness. The very weakness that makes you feel
ashamed, the weakness that you curse, makes you a signpost pointing to the Truth. If you allow it, your weakness can transform your

day-to-day existence into a living gospel message.
So don't curse your powerlessness.
The power you need
   —the power I have given you in my Holy Spirit—
      is the power to grasp the
            width, length, height, and depth
              of the love of Christ.[5]

[1]2 Corinthians 9:8; [2]2 Corinthians 3:18; [3]2 Corinthians 12:9;
[4]2 Corinthians 4:7-8; [5]Ephesians 3:17

13 Mountains into Roads

He who has compassion on them will guide them... I will turn all my mountains into roads....

Isaiah 49:10-11

Your busyness has become my rival.
But you have already sensed that, haven't you?
Slow down, my child, before you plunge headlong
into a ravine cunningly placed in front of you
by the Enemy of your soul.
Satan knows that well-placed mountains and ravines
are the way to distract and hinder you
from your intent to walk in my Way.

I redeemed you and made you holy. I called you to my level road.[1] I will keep you from falling.[2]

I will hedge you in and keep you from aimless wandering.[3] I will keep your feet on the road that leads into my presence.

On the last day I will meet you at the gate shouting,
"Welcome!
Come through the gate, come through![4]
Come under my banner of love."[5]
And you will run through it with great joy.
Never again will you know sorrow or frustration.[6]

My straight path is Jesus Christ.[7]
He makes the rough spots smooth.[8]
Put aside your frenzied activity.
Let your heavy pack slip from your back.[9]
Come to rest in green meadows beside cool,
refreshing waters.
Let me refresh and restore you.[10]

[1]Proverbs 4:26; [2]Jude 24-25; [3]Isaiah 35:8-9; [4]Isaiah 62:10; [5]Song of Solomon 2:4; [6]Isaiah 35:10; [7]John 14:6; [8]Isaiah 40:3-5; [9]Matthew 11:28-30; [10]Psalms 23

14 ᔥ My Unending Love

*I will betroth you to me forever; I will betroth you in right-
eousness and justice, in love and compassion. I will betroth
you in faithfulness, and you will acknowledge the Lord.*
Hosea 2:19-20

Come,
　celebrate my love for you
　as a bride celebrates her marriage.
Rejoice in your salvation
　as I rejoice over you.[1]
I...
I am your knight on a white horse.[2]
I have carried you away into eternal life.
Receive my love—my very Self—with joy,
　as a bride receives her husband.
I have bought you and claimed you as my own.[3]
I have already purchased your wedding gown.
I will exchange your impurity for purity,
　your soiled clothing for white linen, bright and clean![4]
Your place at the Wedding Feast is assured.
Do not attempt to veil your face from me,
　newly conscious of your failings.
My love covers every failure.[5]
It is my love that purifies you and makes you holy...
　my love that will carry you into glory.
It is my mercy that exposes your weakness...
　and your weakness that brings you to my side
　ready to be enveloped in my holy, protective embrace.
Remain in my arms.
Prove my grace sufficient!
There is nothing you must do—nor can you—to earn my love.

My love is unending,
   unchanging, and
   utterly unrestrained.

Put aside your failure and regret. Your resolve to do better cannot buy intimacy with me. All your promises and determination are no match for my fierce love. So rest in my love. Trust that I love you too much to allow your weakness and failures to keep you from me.

I...

I am the Lord your God.

I will never leave you nor forsake you.[6]

[1]Isaiah 62:5b; [2]Revelation 19:11-16; [3]1 Corinthians 6:19-20; [4]Revelation 19:7-8; [5]James 5:20; [6]Joshua 1:5-9

15 ✷ Faith for Now and Eternity

Surely goodness and mercy shall follow me all the days of
my life; and I will dwell in the house of the Lord forever.
Psalm 23:6, NKJV

Call to me out of the wellspring of your faith
  and I will answer.[1]
Pay close attention to my promises;
  study them with a glad heart and receptive mind,
  for they shape the faith
  that springs from my Spirit
  which dwells within you.[2]

Faith recognizes my goodness and mercy, turning your life to sail
  with the current of my love so that all you do, think, and feel
  flows from my promises.
Faith knows my voice, understands my intentions, yields to my
  will.[3]
Faith is certain even of the (as yet) unseen fulfillment of my every
  promise because
  faith trusts in me, hopes in me.[4]
Faith understands that I will never stain my robe or tarnish my
  crown with deception. What I say is perfectly sure. My promises
  stand for all time.

How can doubt survive the fierce proof of the Cross? If I did not
withhold my own Son, but sacrificed him for the sake of the fulfillment of my promises, where is there room for doubt?[5]

You are mine. I have set my angels to stand guard over you.[6] My
goodness and mercy undergird every event in your life, every experience—triumphant or (seemingly) disastrous.

Live with confidence in the security of my promises! Live *for* me
now and *with* me forever.

[1]Psalms 145:17-19; [2]John 14:17; Ephesians 3:14-21; [3]Hebrews
10:19-23; [4]Hebrews 11:1-2; [5]Romans 8:32; [6]Psalms 91:9-12

16 ❧ When You Feel Unloved

For I am convinced that neither death nor life, neither
angels nor demons, neither the present nor the future, nor
any powers, neither height nor depth, nor anything else in
all creation, will be able to separate us from the love of
God that is in Christ Jesus our Lord.

Romans 8:38-39

My love is all-encompassing.

It reaches to you wherever you are.

You will find my love if you search for it in the heavens. You will
find it if you search in the depths. If you rise at the first sign of light
or cross the sea to the other shore, even there my loving hand will
guide you, my right hand will hold you tightly to me.[1]

I *am* Love. Where I am, my love is also.[2]

Once you claim me as your Lord, even the darkness of sin and the
schemes of demons cannot separate you from my unconditional
love.

Nothing.

No, nothing

can separate you from my love.

I created the entire universe.

All of creation is mine to command.

None of it can stand between you and my passionate love.

Nothing.

No, nothing

can separate you from my love.

I bade my Son die so that I might hold you in my embrace and
rock you in my arms as a loving father.

I bade him die so that my Holy Spirit could whisper my truths in
your ears like a lullaby.

I let him go so that I would never have to let go of you.[3]

Nothing.

No, nothing

can separate you from my love.

What is time to me?
I am not bound by time.
I see all of history NOW.
I see Adam being formed of dust right now.
I see my son at Calvary right now.
I see you at the bridal banquet right now.
I see you exchanging your soiled clothing for white robes, your
earthly body for an imperishable one, right now.[4]
It is impossible for you to be separated from my love,
not by your past,
not by your present,
not by your future.
Run into my embrace right now!
Be convinced, my precious child.[5]
Hold fast to the truth of my love.

[1]Psalms 139:8-12; [2]1 John 4:16; [3]1 Thessalonians 4:13-18; [4]Revelation 7:13-17; [5]2 Timothy 1:12

48

17 ↣ Unwavering Hope

Let us hold unswervingly to the hope we profess, for he who promised is faithful.

Hebrews 10:23

You may safely build your hope upon the Rock of my promises,[1]
  for my promises are eternal
  and so is my love.
As long as the sun and moon make their appointed circuits,
  as long as night follows day,
  as long as the stars hang suspended
  in the night sky
  and the sun gives warmth and light,
  so long will my promises toward you remain unchanged.[2]
My love for you is steadfast.
Count the many ways I have demonstrated my love for you.
Count the ways I have delivered you.
Base your faith in me upon my faithfulness throughout your life
  ... throughout all of history.
Then place your hope,
  as a crowning jewel,
  upon your faith.
For faith makes the way for hope.
Faith is a quiet assurance that you will receive what you hope for;
  it's being certain that what I have promised will happen.[3]
You know that I formed the universe.
At my command, visible things were formed from invisible.[4]
The creation itself is testimony to my power...
  my magnificence...
  my faithfulness.[5]

Remain unswervingly on the path of hope. Don't be afraid. Let my hope within you guide your steps. I will equip and enable you to follow me. All the strength and power you need are in my hands.[6] Ask me and they are yours.[7]

[1]Psalms 18:2; 40:2; 61:2; 92:15; [2]Jeremiah 33:19-26; [3]Hebrews 11:1; [4]Hebrews 11:3; [5]Psalms 119:89-90; [6]1 Chronicles 29:11-13; [7]2 Chronicles 16:9a

18 Ꮙᎀ In Challenging Times

Such is the confidence that we have through Christ toward God.
Not that we are competent of ourselves to claim anything as
coming from us; our competence is from God, who has made us
competent to be ministers of the new covenant, not in a written
code but in the Spirit; for the written code kills, but the Spirit
gives life.   **2 Corinthians 3:4-6, RSV**

You're worried because you're not equal to the challenge you face.
My precious child, that's precisely the point. Why should that dis-
tress you? The just live by *faith*. You know where to turn for help.
Why pause to wonder? You can approach any challenge with confidence in *my* strength… in *my* competence.

Ah, yes. You forgot that for a moment, didn't you? Surely you
know that you are not alone in your trouble.

I have promised that I will never turn away from you.
I have promised to make every circumstance
    work toward your ultimate good.[1]
I have a purpose and plan for your life
    that reaches beyond your immediate state.
Trust my plan, even in these circumstances.

Some trust in their possessions, some in their family and friends,[2]
but you… you are called to trust in me. Don't be afraid.[3] You will
not be put to shame.[4]

The law that was written on tablets of stone killed hope because
it merely demonstrated that my holiness is complete and uncompromising; no one can ever meet my standard of holiness.

But my Holy Spirit
    not only writes my law upon your heart,[5]
        he empowers and equips you
            to meet every challenge,
                to obey my law,[6]
                    giving life to your hope to be holy
                      (as I am holy).[7]

You can meet this challenge. You can do all things with and through my strength, which resides in you.[8]

[1]Jeremiah 32:40; Romans 8:28; [2]Psalms 20:7; [3]Psalms 27; Psalms 46; [4]Romans 10:11; [5]Jeremiah 31:33; [6]Isaiah 43:1-5; John 17; [7]Leviticus 11:44-45; 1 Peter 1:16; [8]Philippians 4:13

19 ᴥ When You Don't Know What to Do

I will lead the blind by ways they have not known, along unfamiliar paths I will guide them; I will turn the darkness into light before them and make the rough places smooth.

Isaiah 42:16

You feel unsure, unsafe—blinded by the neon-colored choices offered by the world.[1] Those worldly choices are familiar to you. My paths are not so familiar... yet. You are afraid you will stumble and be hurt if you try my less familiar path. My lovely child, the only thing that can hurt you is disobedience.

I have promised to shine a light on your path and direct your feet when you choose my way over the ways of the world.[2] I will help you. I never desert the humble but guide them with my loving hand.[3] I will accompany you beside cool, clear waters and guide you along safe paths so that your life will be a testimony to my goodness and mercy.[4]

Just think about what I have *already* done for you. In obedience to me my Son set aside his glory and became fully human.[5] He purchased your redemption by giving up his life because it brings me such joy to call you mine.[6] If you needed one hundred times more help and guidance, it would still be a small thing for me![7]

You are afraid that if you start out along an unfamiliar path you will get lost and stray from my side, or worse still, you will grow weary or frightened and deliberately depart from the path. Dear one, *nothing* can separate you from me and I will not allow you to face more than I have prepared you to endure.[8]

I will smooth the road for you. I will give you guidance and protection along the way.[9] And when, in my wisdom, I place your feet on rough and rocky paths, I will make your feet like deer's feet. I will give you strength and enable you to walk in high and winding places without falling.[10]

[1]Colossians 2:6-10; [2]Psalms 119:105; Proverbs 3:5,6; [3]Psalms 25:9-10; [4]Psalms 23; Isaiah 49:10-11; [5]Philippians 2:6-11; [6]Romans 8:15-17; Hebrews 12:2; [7]Romans 8:32; [8]Psalms 139:9, 10; Romans 8:35-39; 1 Corinthians 10:13; [9]Psalms 32:8; [10]Habakkuk 3:18- 19

20 ᧞ When You Lack Direction

The God who made the world and everything in it is the Lord of heaven and earth.... From one man he made every nation of men, that they should inhabit the whole earth; and he determined the times set for them and the exact places where they should live.

Acts 17:24, 27

Let me gather you into my arms
before night falls in the wilderness of your thoughts.
You have wandered long in that wilderness.
Come away. Place your hand in mine and come away with me.
Have no fear. I am in control.
When the path is unfamiliar, I will lead you.
I will shine light in the dark places and keep you
from stumbling.
I will never leave you.[1]
If you lose your way,
I will call you back so that you suffer no harm.[2]
Do not fear.
You cannot stumble into a place too dark for me to find you.
I will guide and protect you
whether you are on the moon or at the bottom of the sea.
Across the ocean or in your own bed,
there is nowhere you can be lost to me.[3]
I have planned every moment of your life;
every beat of your heart, every breath you take, is by my decree.[4]
Banish confusion, come away from the dark and isolated places in
your thoughts. I will help you so that you will not suffer shame.[5]

I chose the exact time in history when you should be born and devised the place in all the earth where you would live. Your circumstances are all under my control. Don't try to muddle through on your own. Turn your heart wholly toward me and trust me, and I will point the way. I will give you direction.[6]

[1]Isaiah 42:16; [2]Isaiah 30:21; [3]Psalms 139:7-12; [4]Psalms 139:13-16; Acts 17:28; [5]Isaiah 50:7 [6]Proverbs 3:5-6

21 ✣ Glory in My Strength

This poor man cried out, and the Lord heard him, and saved him out of all his troubles. The angel of the Lord encamps all around those who fear him, and delivers them. Oh, taste and see that the Lord is good; blessed is the man who trusts in him!

Psalms 34:6-8, NKJV

Cry out to me,
  you who know that your power
  is too poor to save yourself.
I dispatch my angels to care for all my chosen ones.[1]
You are precious to me,
  right down to the tiniest cell in your body.[2]
You are the apple of my eye.[3]
Cry out to me and I will hear you
  and save you from your troubles.[4]
I have marked off an encampment
  —a habitation for my angels—
  around each one who has a right relationship with me.
One day, when your spiritual eyes are opened,
  you will see them there
  —thousands of them—
  standing at the ready with flaming transport.[5]

And if, for the moment, you lack a right relationship with me, do not despair—repent. My angels still fly with live coals from my altar with which to touch your lips and purify you of all guilt so that legions of angels may rejoice.[6]

Trust in me and be blessed.
I will never abandon those who look to me for safety.[7]
Even now I bend my ear to you
  and listen for your slightest whisper.
When Satan schemes against you,

I expose his plans and snatch you from his net.
I will shame your Enemy and set your feet in a place of honor.[8]

[1]Hebrews 1:14; [2]Psalms 72:14; Matthew 10:30; [3]Deuteronomy 32:10; [4]Psalms 72:12; [5]2 Kings 6:8-17; Psalms 68:17; [6]Isaiah 6:1-8; Luke 15:10; [7]Psalms 9:9-10; [8]Psalms 31

22 ᕽ No Other Name

These things I have written to you who have believed in the name of the Son of God, in order that you may know that you have eternal life. And this is the confidence which we have before him, that, if we ask anything according to his will, he hears us. And if we know that he hears us in whatever we ask, we know that we have the requests which we have asked from him.

1 John 5:13-15, NASB

I am your Father-God. You are precious to me. I planned you from the beginning of time. I watched you grow within your mother's womb.[1] Your first smile made *me* smile. I watched you with delight for hours as you explored the tastes, sounds, and feel of your surroundings. I treasure the memory of your first step. The sound of your first laugh is stored in my heart for all time. My affection for you is deep and enduring.[2]

I am your Father-God. You may enter my presence fully confident. Like the father of a wandering son, I welcome you into my presence with joy and happily restore you to complete fellowship when you have strayed from my side.[3]

To ensure that you are capable of doing all that I have called you to do, I have given you the full exercise of the authority of that name which is above all other names, Jesus Christ.[4]

Let no one steal your joy. I have furnished you with all you need in order to do all that I require.[5] My commands are also my promise of victory! (I would not command it if it were not possible.)[6]

When you pray, pray with expectation—absolutely certain of my answer.[7] I hear the prayers of one who is right with me.[8] Then nothing is impossible, nothing is out of your reach.[9]

I am your Father-God. Come and worship me. Continually abide in my presence. Declare my grandeur and humbly accept my right to rule over your life, because I have made you complete, altogether holy, lacking nothing.[10]

¹Psalms 139:13-16; ²Psalms 136; ³Luke 15:11-32; ⁴John 14:12-14; Acts 4:8-12; Philippians 2:1-11; 1 John 5:14-15; ⁵John 16:19-24; ⁶Philippians 4:13; ⁷Psalms 5:3; ⁸Proverbs 15:29; ⁹Matthew 17:20; ¹⁰2 Corinthians 3:18; Philippians 1:6; 1 Peter 1:15-16; 5:6

PART TWO

God's Promise
Fulfilled in Us

23 ᔧ So That You May Believe

He who did not spare his own Son, but gave him up for us all—how will he not also, along with him, graciously give us all things?

Romans 8:32

I am the giver of every certain promise. I have sealed my promises with my royal signet, dipped in priestly blood. My promises flow from my holy and unchanging grace as a token of my great love for you.

Let your faith be born and sustained by these truths:

I have all power.

Nothing and no one is more powerful than I.

I am unchanging.

From before I set the cosmic clock
—marking off the seconds since creation—
until the day it ticks its final second
and beyond,
I am who I am.

I gave my promises so that men and women might believe them, receive them, and praise me.

I created and completed
the greatest of all promises—salvation.[1]

I have already fulfilled that promise in your life.

If I have fulfilled that most costly of promises,
how can you doubt that I will fulfill all of my other promises
when you claim them from your place within my plan?[2]

I am not a stingy father. You were specially chosen to rule with Christ as a member of the royal priesthood.[3] All of the King's riches belong to his children.[4] Those riches were purchased for you at great personal expense—shame and death for my firstborn—yet I considered you worth such a high price, both then and now.[5]

Claim the promises of your generous Father and King.

[1]Hebrews 12:1-2; [2]James 4:2-3; [3]Ephesians 2:4-10; 1 Peter 2:9; [4]Romans 8:28-31; Hebrews 1; 1 Corinthians 3:23; [5]Isaiah 52-53; Philippians 2:6-11

24 ❧ Hope Born of Righteousness

By faith we eagerly await through the Spirit the righteousness for which we hope. For in Christ Jesus neither circumcision nor uncircumcision has any value. The only thing that counts is faith expressing itself through love.

Galatians 5:5-6

Place your hope in me, my little one;
  for what I have promised,
I am faithful to accomplish.
I have promised to complete my glorifying work in you,
  and I will do it![1]
When you stand before me on the last day,
  you will be clothed in innocence...[2]
  and acquitted of every charge brought against you.[3]
  My uncompromising law
  —and the impossible task of fulfilling it—
  no longer has you in its grip.

You can be absolutely secure in your hope that Christ's virtuous life, death, and resurrection—all undergone on your behalf—have paid the price for your wrongdoing.[4]
Such a hope can never disappoint.

Just as I am faithful, my Spirit is also faithful,
  enabling you to express your faith through love
      because I have poured out my love into your heart
        through my Holy Spirit.[5]
          I have written my law upon your heart.[6]

My Holy Spirit equips you to place the interests of others before your own,[7] to love them as you would like to be loved.[8]
Do not worry about failing me. You will naturally express your faith through love...
  as you abide in me.

As you prayerfully rest in my arms
   you will find the petty concerns of this life fading away, replaced
   by a genuine love and concern for my people
   and my work.[9]

I have given you the strength and the means to overcome this world and the lure of its interests. Lean on that hope and forge ahead fearlessly.

[1]Philippians 1:6; [2]Revelation 7:9-12; [3]Isaiah 54:16-17; [4]Acts 13:38-39; [5]Romans 5:5; [6]2 Corinthians 3:3; [7]Philippians 2:1-11; [8]Romans 13:9-10; [9]John 15:5

25 ∾ When Obedience Is Difficult

*I will bind you to me forever with chains of righteousness
and justice and love and mercy.*

Hosea 2:19, TLB

My precious child, I understand your struggle. It is human to seek
what seems to be the easy road.

Self-sacrifice seems so tiresome and unpleasant.

You strain at my restraints, don't you? You hunger for independence. You want to be "free."

Yet you have found yourself peering into some awfully dark places
in your search for freedom. If you strive to be independent, to
be free from all restraints, you will merely tighten the chains you
wear, becoming enslaved to your own desires.

Your old nature was rendered powerless, being crucified with Christ
the instant you believed unto salvation. You are no longer a slave
to sin.[1]

My Son has set you utterly free![2]

I want to exchange your chains for
my chains of righteousness, justice, love, and mercy.

Rather than being heavy and cumbersome,
my burden is light.[3]

My chains offer true freedom,
the freedom for which I *created* you,
the freedom to choose what is right.

So take my chains upon you and learn from me
so that you may find rest for your soul.

When you exchange your independence and "freedom" for
absolute dependence and obedience, you will enjoy true freedom—the freedom to be all you are meant to be.

[1]Romans 6:6-7; [2]John 8:36; [3]Matthew 11:29-30

26 ❧ You Are Holy and Blameless

For he chose us in him before the creation of the world to be holy and blameless in his sight.

Ephesians 1:4

Little one, you are bent under a terrible load of guilt and shame. You have gathered all your mistakes and shortcomings in a bundle,
   dragging it
       behind you
           by a tether of
              regret.

The tether tangles around your feet, tripping you, preventing you from entering fully into my joy.

Did I not create you to be holy and blameless? Have I not promised to keep you radiantly free from shame when you place your hope in me?[1]

Don't be like those who try to prove their worthiness by petting their guilt and caressing their shame,
   clutching their bundle to them
   in an effort to prove their contrition,
   as if to earn my forgiveness.

There are only two choices—and
   earning my forgiveness
   is not one of them.

You may clutch your bundle and accept the consequences,
   or you may confess your shortcomings to me
   and allow me to remove them from you
   as far as the east is
   from the west.[2]

Then I will forgive and bless you with peace, courage, love, and self-discipline.[3] Why carry your load another step? Will you accept my free gift, leave your bundle at my feet, and walk away?

[1]Psalms 34:5; 69:6; [2]Psalms 103:12; [3]Psalms 29:11; 2 Timothy 1:7

27 ❧ Light That Gleams through Darkness

The effective, fervent prayer of [the] righteous… avails much.

James 5:16, NKJV

I watch you knocking on every door (but mine)… searching, needy. Mine is the final door on your appointed rounds. You arrive—breathless and tearful—only when worry and desperation drive you there. Although I have flung wide the door to my riches and power, you travel every other road before approaching the light that gleams from my open door, penetrating the darkness.

You say you do not ask because I may not answer. Dear one, I always answer. Ask from righteous motives and my answer will always please you.[1]

You say you do not ask because I may take "too long." What look like delays from your perspective are, from my perspective, faith-building, grace-growing experiences. Delays may exercise your humility more than you would prefer for comfort's sake but, I promise you, when you have a need, I will meet it—guaranteed.[2] If you don't receive, it is because you do not need.

When you have a need, do not waste a single instant worrying; remove your white robe from the twin hooks of confession and repentance, put it on, enter my throne room, and ask me.[3]

Sometimes you do not ask because you are "saving" your petitions for more "important" things. You are actually afraid I may grow tired of hearing your voice. Not true, my dearly beloved child![4] Giving you your heart's desire delights me beyond measure.

Pray to me constantly—from the moment you open your eyes in the morning until you pass through slumber's veil at night.[5] Adorned with a clear conscience and godly desires, ask boldly, believing that I have the power and willingness to accomplish what you ask.[6] Make passionate, daring requests. Ask, and keep asking. I will answer.[7]

[1]James 4:3; [2]James 4:10; [3]James 5:16a; Philippians 4:6; [4]Mark 11:22-26; [5]1 Thessalonians 5:17; Philippians 4:4-7; Psalms 5:1-3; [6]Matthew 21:21-22; [7]Luke 11:5-13

28 ❧ Greatest in the Kingdom

I tell you the truth, unless you change and become like little children, you will never enter the kingdom of heaven. Therefore, whoever humbles himself like this child is greatest in the kingdom of heaven.

Matthew 18:3-4

The wonders of childhood are some of humanity's best kept secrets, despite the fact that they are treasures stored right out in the open. It's because they seem so insignificant—as if they aren't treasures at all—that no one bothers with them.

I can see I have your attention now. You want to know these
    secrets, don't you?
To a child, the world is a wondrous place.[1]
Children's senses are attuned to the world around them.
They are not invested in seeming competent and proper.
They do not even understand the concepts.
They know nothing of pride and self-sufficiency.
They know only humility and dependence.
Children soak up all the beauty in creation
    and automatically perceive
    that the Creator of all that beauty must be
Someone awesome.[2]
That's why faith comes so easily to children.
Who wouldn't have absolute,
    unquestioning faith
    in the Creator of all that wonderful "stuff"?[3]

You have allowed your responsibilities to hem you in. Busyness chokes off your senses. Your mind has raced away, carrying your capacity for wonder with it.

Think about it. There are few things more relaxing than feeling awed. What happens when you look at a snow-capped mountain? When you stop to listen to the hushed rustling of leaves and small animals in a beautiful forest? You take a deep breath, tension drains from your muscles, and your capacity for worship is restored.[4]

When I call you my child it isn't just a figure of speech. It is reality. You have the ability—and my permission—to come out and play.

Claim childlike humility again.
　　Trust me as only a child can trust.[5]
　　　　Grasp my hand and walk with me.
　　　　　　Tune in all of your senses.
　　　　　　　　Be prepared to be awestruck
　　　　　　　　　　... and worshipful!

[1]Job 37:14-18; [2]Psalms 89:5-8; [3]Deuteronomy 10:21; [4]Psalms 65; [5]Mark 9:24

29 ✌ When You Feel Defeated by Sin

*I will give you a new heart and put a new spirit in you; I
will remove from you your heart of stone and give you a
heart of flesh. And I will put my Spirit in you and move
you to follow my decrees and be careful to keep my laws.…
You will be my people, and I will be your God. I will save
you from all your uncleanness.*

Ezekiel 36:26-29a

Be at peace, my lovely child.
You have not failed me beyond redemption.
Your stinging conscience proves that.

Still, you are right to seek me. All is not well with you. Confess
your shortcomings to me, dear one, and receive my forgiveness
with joy so that all may be well once more.

You find it difficult, I know, to understand how it could be that
easy. You reach for some more complicated process for restoring
your relationship with me. You ask—again—how a simple admis-
sion of guilt can have power. It has power because I have commanded that it be so. Why do you look for a more complicated
answer?

You know from previous experience that when you grasp for
something more, your hand closes around empty air.

I am perfect,
   utterly holy,
      and absolutely powerful.
         I am well able to make you holy.[1]
           And I have promised to do so.[2]
Just as I have reached to the core of your being
   and placed my Spirit in you,
      giving you a heart of flesh,
         bringing you into my kingdom,[3]
         making you my own,[4]
   so too, will I continue the work of making you holy.[5]

It is human to want to escape from pain, but don't be afraid of *this* heartache. Rather, rejoice and be glad. You are not defeated... because *I* am not defeated. It is my Spirit in you who pricks your conscience and makes your heart ache, fueling your desire to live by my principles.

Run to me.
Place your aching heart in my hands,
a warm and living sacrifice.[6]

Trust that I will use your heartache to shape you into a holy, obedient child. Trust me to redeem your pain and sadness and give you life![7]

[1]Isaiah 6:3-8; [2]Romans 6:6-11; [3]Colossians 1:13; [4]1 Corinthians 6:19-20; [5]Philippians 1:6; [6]Romans 12:1-2; [7]Romans 6:13-14

30 ↝ Forgiveness Is Yours

For as high as the heavens are above the earth, so great is
his love for those who fear him; as far as the east is from the
west, so far has he removed our transgressions from us.
Psalms 103:11-12

Look up, my child!
Even the sky overhead
   is too puny to encompass
   the vastness of my love for you.
Why do you chase after my forgiveness
   as if you must wrest it from my unwilling grip
   through sheer determination and frenzied activity?
Your Enemy whispers condemnation in your ear.
He wants you to feel unforgiven and unacceptable.
But you have turned from your wrongdoing
   with a repentant heart
   and my forgiveness is already yours.[1]

If you head east around the globe will you eventually find yourself going west? Impossible! East and west will never meet; they are
separated for all time.
   So it is with you and your sins.
   Cease your struggles and rest in my love.[2]

For my sake I have wiped away
   every wrong you ever committed.
      I no longer remember the slightest one.[3]

My son, Jesus Christ, came into the world to provide absolute
forgiveness even for the worst sinner.[4] Your ugliest sin can be
expunged by his unparalleled sacrifice.

Do not say, "Yes, but that doesn't... can't... mean me." My love is so great, so all-encompassing, that I sent my Son to die for people who had no hope of ever being anything but sinners.[5] Does that describe you?

Become deaf to your Enemy's accusations! Don't give him a foothold. Forget the past, live in the present, and look forward to the future. Fix your eyes on the One who calls you toward your heavenly goal and be at peace.[6]

[1]2 Samuel 11:1-12:13; [2]Isaiah 30:15a,b; [3]Isaiah 43:25; [4]1 Timothy 1:15-16; [5]Romans 5:8; [6]Philippians 3:13-14; Isaiah 26:3-4

31 ☞ Walking through the Fire

Fear not, for I have redeemed you; I have called you by name;
you are mine. When you pass through the waters, I will be with
you; and when you pass through the rivers, they will not sweep
over you. When you walk through the fire, you will not be
burned....

Isaiah 43:1-2

I have claimed you for my own and I jealously keep watch over you.[1] I would not consider, for the slightest fraction of a second, allowing Satan to claim you back from me. You are mine! He can never have you.[2] So put away thoughts of abandonment. The fact that you must endure trials is not proof of my faltering. I love you as much now as I did when I named you, before I molded the earth with my hands or dusted the night sky with diamonds. I will not abandon you in your sufferings.[3]

Yes, I named you, as any loving Father would. The name I gave you testifies to your heritage—a new nature and holy desires that are a reflection of your Father. I have already inscribed your new name on a white stone—a symbol of the innocence attributed to you the moment you believed.[4]

When you are facing a flood of life's troubles,
    when flames of worldly evils dance around you,
        look to me in faith.

Do not rely on the world's ways of dealing with adversity.

You have a far more impressive array of weaponry at hand. I have given you the power to crush even Satan's forces.

Therefore, refuse to pay attention when your imagination conjures pictures of every awful possibility that might overtake you in this trial. Refuse to believe those who would tell you that your faith in me is no match for your fate. Teach your thoughts to obey, make them attend to the lessons in my Word.[5] Believe in my love. Rely on me to carry you through the flood. Trust me to shelter you from the flames.

[1]1 Samuel 2:9; Isaiah 52:12; [2]John 3:16; [3]Hebrews 1:10-14;
[4]Revelation 2:17; Ephesians 2:8-9; [5]2 Corinthians 10:3-5

32 ✨ God's Plans for You

*"For I know the plans I have for you," declares the Lord, "plans
to prosper you and not to harm you, plans to give you hope and a
future. Then you will call upon me and come and pray to me,
and I will listen to you. You will seek me and find me when you
seek me with all of your heart."*

Jeremiah 29:11-13

I see your downcast spirit, my beloved child. Your hope has
flown away on the wings of your cares. Fear has pulled up a chair in
your heart and planned to stay awhile.

Quickly now—
pausing to reason with it will only extend its stay—
you must treat it like any uninvited,
destructive,
ill-tempered guest
and send it away![1]

What is it about your future that seems so daunting? The wonder and adventure of discovering the unknown? Or perhaps the
endless possibilities? Ah, but yes. You see those possibilities as grim,
foreboding creatures set to leap out at you from the dark, don't
you?

Dear one, you can't imagine the glorious plans I have for your
future. I have planted in you the desire to seek me with all your
heart. And when you seek me, you will find me. You can be sure of
that. You can be sure of *all* my promises.

I plan to make your spirit grow in wisdom and understanding,
because, when your heart is wise, you will be filled with gladness
and your future filled with hope.[2]

There is no need to worry. My plans for you have been in place
from the beginning—many ages before you were conceived—
harmonizing with the plans I have established for the entire universe.[3] No one and nothing can prevent my plans for you from

being realized right down to the last detail.[4] My plans stand—unchanging and unchangeable—forever.[5]

So call upon me, come and pray to me. I promise to listen. Seek me. You will find me. And I will carry you into your exciting, unknown future—a future meant for your good.

[1] John 4:18; Isaiah 43:1-2; Jeremiah 17:8; [2]Proverbs 23:15-18; [3]Ephesians 1:11; [4]Job 42:2; [5]Psalms 33:11

33 ✦ Justified through Faith

Therefore, since we have been justified through faith, we have peace with God through our Lord Jesus Christ, through whom we have gained access by faith into this grace in which we now stand.

Romans 5:1-2

Stand before me, my little one, eyes shining in my reflected glory.
Your salvation is the culmination of my plan.[1]
You are my masterpiece.[2]

    Your faith has plunged you
        into the cleansing flood of
            Christ's innocence,
      washing you clean so that your sins
   —though they were bright as scarlet—
are washed as white as snow.[3]

It is my gift of faith
   —planted and nurtured within your heart,
   purchased by my Son, Jesus Christ—
   that opened the door to my throne room
   so that you may stand in my presence without fear.
Hold your head high, my precious child.
Gaze into my eyes and
   see the fire of my burning love for you.[4]
Stand before me—unafraid.
Allow the peace of Christ to govern your heart, teaching it to bend
   to my will in joy and thanksgiving.[5]
My plans are for your good.[6]
I have turned my face toward you.
I have raised my scepter to welcome you into my presence.[7]
I will shower you with blessings and keep you safe from harm.
My grace flows over and around you.

It holds you up and hedges you in,
   so that you may live in peace with me forever.[8]

[1]Romans 16:25-27; [2]Ephesians 2:10; [3]Isaiah 1:18; [4]Deuteronomy 11:12; 2 Chronicles 16:9a; Psalms 101:6; [5]Colossians 3:15; [6]Jeremiah 29:11-13; [7]Esther 4:11-5:2; [8]Numbers 6:24-26

34 ✀ God's Mark of Innocence

God is light; in him there is no darkness at all.... and the blood of Jesus, his Son, purifies us from all sin.

1 John 1:5, 7

Because of my mercy, compassion, and unfailing love, all of your wrong acts, thoughts, and words are blotted out, washed away in the cleansing flood flowing from the cross.[1]
You were freed, once and for all,
    the day you believed.
You are being freed day by day,
    (every time you confess and repent)
    and you will be freed—tomorrow,
    and the next day,
    and the day after that.
Christ's work of purification is finished.[2]
There is nothing more to be done.
Renounce the forlorn hope of
    forgiveness yet to be earned.
Forgiveness is yours *now*,
    free and clear!
What's more, my forgiveness is complete and all-encompassing.
    You are purified from *all* your sins... so spotless that I—the
    Holy One—have taken up residence within you.[3]

Living fountains of water rush from your heart,
    completely untainted,
        crystalline...
                glistening in the reflected brilliance of the Son.[4]

Your sins may be many and bitter.
They may be numerous enough to fill the sea itself
    with crashing breakers of guilt.
Yet my Son's blood is adequate to cleanse them all,
    to wipe away every guilty drop
        with nothing left to show that they were ever there.[5]

No one can bring a charge against you. You are absolved of all wrong, you bear my mark for all time. You are marked "Innocent."[6]

[1]Psalms 51:1; [2]John 19:30; [3]Isaiah 6:1-7; 1 Peter 1:15-16; 1 Corinthians 3:16; [4]John 7:37-38; [5]Isaiah 1:18; [6]Romans 8:33

35 ☙ God's Lavish Love

*Yet to all who received him, to those who believed in his
name, he gave the right to become children of God.*
John 1:12-13

You're surprised by the intensity of my love. You have not yet
grasped the magnitude of my adoption plan
    ... the extraordinary price I paid
    to claim you.[1]
In obedience to me, my Son
    —who was and is equal with me—
    gave up the glory and honor of heaven
    to become human.
He was tortured and murdered, and his blood spilled on the
    ground like that of a common animal.
All in payment for you.[2]

What's more...
I set the price myself!
That's how valuable you are to me.[3]
That's how much I wanted to spend eternity
    lavishing my love on you.
That's how much I wanted to call you my child.
And that is what you are—my child![4]
Yet you draw back from me. You still fall prey to the notion that
    your sins are too great to be paid for
    by my Son's blood.
My child, when you dwell on your feelings of guilt,
    when you continue to assert your unworthiness,
    you are actually denying the legitimacy
    of your adoption.
Don't let that happen.
You have been absolved of all wrongdoing and declared
    my child.[5]

Your false guilt gives you many reasons to worry. You worry about all kinds of circumstances. You worry about money and security. You concern yourself with hair, and food, and fashion. But circumstances are no match for me. Look around you, my lovely one. You know how beautiful the flowers and grasses are. They are clothed in a splendor greater than the richest king that ever lived. If I care for them, how can you wonder whether I will care for you?[6]

There is a voice within you that tells you that you are my own true child. Listen to that voice! My Holy Spirit adds his voice to yours, testifying that you are, indeed, my child.[7]

[1]Ephesians 1:4-8; [2]Philippians 2:5-11; [3]Luke 12:7; [4]1 John 3:1; [5]Titus 3:3-8; [6]Matthew 6:25-34; [7]Romans 8:16

36 ~ Times of Refreshing

Let us acknowledge the Lord; let us press on to acknowledge him. As surely as the sun rises, he will appear; he will come to us like the winter rains, like the spring rains that water the earth.

Hosea 6:3

Leap for joy, my child!
Sing and dance with delight!
Revel in the knowledge that your repentant heart pleases me![1]
You have turned your face from sin.
You have turned your heart toward me
    and your soul will be refreshed.[2]
I will restore your soul
    like a gentle rain restores the land.
Your spirit will bloom with the fresh radiance of joy.[3]
Continue on your chosen path, my lovely one, and you will see me
    as surely as the sun appears in the morning.
Praise and celebrate the Lamb![4]
Put away somber ventures for a time!
Take pleasure in what you're doing now! Yes, enjoy life!
It all comes from my hand.[5]
I have empowered you to keep my law. I have tilled the rocky places
    of your heart. I have plowed up the fertile soil so that the seeds
    of my love may burst forth along with the lush fruit of my
    Spirit.[6]
Receive my gift!
Untie the starry ribbon of early morning!
Tear the brightly colored dawn from each day!
Celebrate my daily blessings.
My gift of love and compassion can never be exhausted.
They are faithfully renewed each morning.[7]
Go ahead! Brag that your Father can touch the mountain tops.
Boast of your Father's kindness, justice, and righteousness.[8]

Tell your friends of my great love. Sing and shout your joy in me...
and know that I am pleased.

[1]Ecclesiastes 2:26; [2]Acts 3:19; [3]Hosea 6:3; [4]Revelation 5; [5]James 1:17; [6]Ezekiel 36:26-27; Galatians 5:22-23; [7]Lamentations 3:22-23; [8]Jeremiah 9:24

37 ᕱ A Robe of Righteousness

I delight greatly in the Lord; my soul rejoices in my God.
For he has clothed me with garments of salvation and
arrayed me in a robe of righteousness.

Isaiah 61:10

Put away thoughts of failure.
 Set aside defeat.
  Rejoice in me!
   I have declared you righteous!
I have given you a white robe to wear in my presence. I gave you
such a magnificent robe so that you would be properly clothed to
spend your time with me.
I delight in you.[1]
 I want you to come to my throne room
  boldly and often
   so that you may receive my mercy and grace
    always.[2]
Refuse to depend on yourself to keep your robe clean.
Instead, trust that my Son's cleansing work is complete,
 just as it stands.[3]
The robe I have given you is fashioned from my Son's robe.
It will never soil,
 it will never wear out;
 it is immaculate and imperishable...
 and very, very costly.[4]
So come into my presence with gladness.
Enter through my gates praising and
 singing songs of gratitude for my undying love.
Know that I am the Lord, your Sovereign King.[5]

[1]Psalms 149:4; [2]Hebrews 4:16; [3]Hebrews 9:28; [4]Acts 2:22-24;
[5]Psalms 100

38 ⭗ Overcoming Habits

When God made his promise to Abraham... he swore by
himself.... God did this so that... we who have fled to take
hold of the hope offered to us may be greatly encouraged.
We have this hope as an anchor for our soul, firm and
secure.

Hebrews 6:13-19

You feel such regret that you cringe at the thought of entering my
presence. I'm glad you have come anyway. I treasure your company.

You're surprised by that, aren't you?

My child, you are a precious gem in my treasure trove. You are
among the spoils captured in the victory established by my Son
when he led captives in his triumphant train.[1]

This habit with which you struggle will not defeat you. But you
feel defeated, I know, and you wonder how I can say that.

Look at the facts. You have my Holy Spirit in you, which is the
assurance of an already established victory. Do you really think this
habit you struggle with is too hard for me?[2]

I have given you authority to master this habit, to overthrow all
the power of your Enemy. Nothing will harm you.[3]

There are those close to you who suggest this habit places you
outside of my love.

What utter nonsense!

My love is not that minuscule.

I have chosen you for my own.

I paid your purchase price in blood.[4]

Nothing and no one can steal you from me.[5]

I do want and expect you to work diligently to overcome this
habit, but you are not alone in your efforts. I am at work in you,
always helping you to act in harmony with my will.[6]

Ask for my help and it is yours.[7]

Seek encouragement and hope in my Word, and you will find it.[8]

Trust me to show you how to make my promised victory your personal reality.[9]

Your hope, my precious gem, remains in being anchored to my promises. Then you will always rest in a place of security.

[1]Ephesians 4:7-8; [2]Genesis 18:14a; [3]Luke 10:19; [4]1 Corinthians 6:19-20; [5]John 6:35-40; [6]Philippians 2:12,13; [7]Luke 11:9; [8]Romans 15:4; [9]Proverbs 3:5-6; Psalms 71:14-21

39 ↬ When You Feel Worthless

For it is by grace you have been saved, through faith—and this not from yourselves, it is the gift of God—not by works, so that no one can boast. For we are God's workmanship, created in Christ Jesus to do good works, which God prepared in advance for us to do.

Ephesians 2:8-10

You are mine. You have been bought with a price. You sparkle in my hand like jewels in a crown. Your very body is my dwelling place.[1]

I sealed my Holy Spirit within you
   once and for all
      the instant you believed unto salvation.
Your inheritance—
     the inheritance you are entitled to
        because you are my child—
           is guaranteed.[2]
Your struggle is intense and,
    make no mistake,
        it is life-threatening.
But the wise person values her own soul.[3]

I have already placed a token of your inheritance within you.
I have already planned every task I will ever ask of you.
You already have everything you need in order to do my will.
You are my workmanship.[4]
When you denigrate yourself, you mock me!
You accuse *ME* of poor workmanship.
I take exception to those who speak harshly against you,
   my beloved—
   even when the speaker is you.
That's not the way to use the freedom I have given you.

In Christ you are all that I created you to be
  from the foundation of the world.
You have nothing to prove.
    ... nothing to earn.
There is nothing you can do that will make me love you more.
  There is nothing you can ever do that will make me love you
  less.

[1]1 Corinthians 6:19-20; [2]Ephesians 1:13; 4:30; [3]Proverbs 19:8;
[4]Psalms 139:14; Ephesians 2:10

40 ᔫ Joy in the Morning

Weeping may endure for a night, but joy comes in the morning.

Psalms 30:5, NKJV

Your feet have slipped
   on the sorrows of life.
Your fears add to the gloom that
   seems to have closed around you.
You are afraid I will not deem you
   worthy of rescue.

My cherished child, I never wish to see you suffer unnecessarily. I never deal with you according to your personal holiness (or lack of it).[1] I know that holiness is not within your grasp.
   Holiness stems entirely from my work within you.
   Take my hand, dear one.
   Hold tight.
   Let me draw you from the well of despair.
   You won't be singing any praises to me from there.[2]

Why are you so distressed?[3] My love can reach even to the depths of your despair.[4] Let me gently dry your tears with words of comfort. I am your loving Father. I will deliver you from your troubles, as I have done so often in the past.
   Soon, your troubles will be only a fading memory, bits of flotsam floating past, carried on the current of your life.[5]
   Nothing can truly harm you. Your place with me is secure.[6] Your future is certain. When you have such assurance, what is there to fear?[7]
   When troubles come—whether surprising or predictable—I will keep you safe. I will lift you up out of your troubles. Then your shout of victory will make you smile; you will lift your head to seek

my face once more, and I will sing and laugh with you in celebration.[8]

When it feels as if your life is ebbing, seeping from your wound-
ed heart, bathe your wounds in the healing balm of my Word. My
Word gives life.[9]

[1]Psalms 103:10; [2]Psalms 30:8-9; [3]Psalms 42:5-6; [4]Romans 8:38-39;
[5]Job 11:16; [6]Philippians 3:20; [7]Psalms 27; [8]Psalm 27; [9]Psalms
119:50

41 ✢ Your Ransom Paid

Therefore, if anyone is in Christ, he is a new creation; old things have passed away; behold, all things have become new.

2 Corinthians 5:17, NKJV

Do you understand your position in my Kingdom, my holy child?
Do you truly comprehend what my son did on your behalf?
You are one with my son, Jesus Christ,
 joined with him for all time.
When sin held you prisoner,
 Christ paid your ransom.[1]
When the Accuser seeks to destroy you
 with the truth about your failings,
 Christ overpowers his accusation
 with his self-sacrificing love.[2]

Jesus Christ, the only one who has the right to condemn you for your sin, joined the ranks of sinners instead, so that he might stand with you on the day you must give an account.[3]

Because of my abundant grace toward you, I chose to impart to you my holiness. I sent my son to rescue you from the clutches of the evil prevalent in the old order and—before I created a single corner of the universe—I paused to write your name in my book, claiming you as a member of my kingdom, my new creation.[4]

Still, for you, there exists a mystery. Although you are complete in Christ my work of sanctification is not yet complete in you.[5] How can that be?

You see, becoming a new creation is only the first of many fruits of salvation. You are a new creation by virtue of your salvation, but the firstfruits are not the entire harvest, just as the first work of my Holy Spirit in your life is not its completion. You have yet to reap perfect holiness. Therefore, hunger and thirst for righteousness.[6] Earnestly ask for my abundant grace to be poured into your life.

Crave holiness and fulfill your desire with the diligent study of my Truth.[7]

Use my Word to light your path. Set your heart on obedience,[8] knowing that you *cannot* fail... because you are a new creation.

[1]Job 33:24; [2]Revelation 12:7-12; [3]2 Corinthians 5:21; [4]Ephesians 1:3-14; 1 Corinthians 1:2; Revelation 3:5; [5]Philippians 3:12-14; [6]Matthew 5:6; [7]John 17:17; [8]Psalms 119:105-112

42 ᴦ Feeding on the Bread of Life

Come, all you who are thirsty, come to the waters; and you
who have no money, come, buy and eat!

Isaiah 55:1

Many pay good money to satiate their senses. They spend their
hard-earned cash to feed their hungry souls. They race through
worldly gutters pursuing things that cannot gratify. Yet they over-
look my satisfying Word served with loving care, spread in a tran-
quil meadow.[1]
They feed on cotton candy and pretend it is the Bread of Life.
I'm glad you crave better things.
When you feed upon my wisdom day and night,
>   you eat and are satisfied...
I fulfill the desires of your heart,
>   because your desires are my desires.[2]
Encourage the wrongdoer to race after my Bread.
Sing my praises in her presence.
Tell her the great and wondrous things I have accomplished in your
>   life.[3]
Call her from her place in the gutter.
>   Draw water for her from the well of salvation.[4]
>   Quench her panting thirst with Living Water,
>   free of charge.[5]
Teach her where to drink so that she will never thirst again.[6]
>   Show her how to live for me and I will shower her—and you—
with mercy.[7]
>   Then, watch and be glad as the streams of living water flowing
from your spirits mingle, making you forever-sisters.[8] Rejoice with
the mountains and hills; celebrate, with all of nature, Christ's saving
work within you.[9]

[1]Psalms 23; [2]Isaiah 55:2-3; [3]Isaiah 12:4-5; [4]Isaiah 12:3; [5]Psalms
42:1; [6]John 6:35; Revelation 21:6; 22:17; [7]Isaiah 55:6-7; Daniel
12:3; Hebrews 6:10; [8]John 7:38; [9]Isaiah 55:12

43 ✢ My Devotion to My Children

My help comes from the Lord, the maker of heaven and earth. He will not let your foot slip—he who watches over you will not slumber; indeed, he… will neither slumber nor sleep.

Psalms 121:2-4

Lift your eyes to the heavens
   and meditate on my awesome power;
   call to mind my devotion to you.
Cease looking at your failings and
   look up instead.[1]
Even when foolishness and stubbornness
   momentarily blind you to my will
      I keep you close to me,
         I grasp your hand tightly.[2]

You are continually on my mind.
   I ceaselessly protect you, always planning for your good.[3]
   Because of my magnificent grace toward you
   I have filled you with the righteousness of Christ,
   I have clothed you in his white robes.
You stand holy before me. You occupy a place of privilege.[4]
   My love endures forever.[5]

You rest, safe and secure,
   cradled in my hand.
No one can snatch you away from me.[6]
   I have placed your name
      like a seal over my heart
        so that you are always with me.
          My love for you is strong and inescapable.[7]
Lift your eyes to the heavens and remember
   my great love toward you.

[1]Psalms 121:1; [2]Psalms 73:21-26; [3]Isaiah 49:15-17; [4]1 Corinthians 1:4-9; Ephesians 1:4-6; [5]Psalms 100; [6]John 10:28-29; [7]Song of Songs 8:6-7

44 ❧ Claiming the Hope That's in You

And we, who with unveiled faces all reflect the Lord's glory, are being transformed into his likeness with ever increasing glory, which comes from the Lord, who is the Spirit.

2 Corinthians 3:18

Rejoice, my child,
 for the veil has been removed
  from the eyes of your heart
   so that you may reflect my glory.[1]

When Moses delivered my law, written on tablets of stone, he covered his face because my reflected glory was fading. My glory is reflected even more by my law written on your heart... and *that* glory does not fade![2] It will grow ever brighter until the day my Son comes to carry you away.[3]

Be joyful, my little one. Sing praises to Christ, the fulfillment of the law, who removed the veil from your heart.[4] Through him, you have been released from death into life.[5]

Turn from sadness. Do not accept condemnation.[6] Do not focus on your imperfection; rather, focus on my perfection, which is being revealed in you. It is necessary for my glory to be reflected by your imperfect heart in order to show clearly that this glory is not something you have attained on your own; it is a reflection of a glory that is mine and mine alone.[7]

That is not meant as permission to coddle your imperfections, of course. You are called to struggle with your sinful nature, endeavoring to walk closer—and ever closer—with me. Yet you will not accomplish that nearly so well by focusing on yourself as you will by focusing on me.

Claim this hope which is in you. You are no longer a slave but my child and the recipient of all I have.[8]

Claim this power which is in you. It is an awesome power

comparable to the power I exerted when I raised Christ from the dead.[9]

Give me your full attention and my glory will be made complete in you.[10]

[1]Ephesians 1:17-23; 2 Corinthians 3:7-8; [2]Philippians 1:6; [3]1 Thessalonians 4:13-18; [4]2 Corinthians 3:14; [5]Romans 6:13; [6]Romans 8:1; [7]2 Corinthians 4:7; [8]Galatians 4:7; [9]Ephesians 1:18-20; [10]Matthew 6:33

❧

PART THREE

God's Promise
to Perfect Us

45 ᔥ The Tempering of Your Soul

*And the God of grace, who called you to his eternal glory
in Christ, after you have suffered a little while, will himself restore you and make you strong, firm and steadfast.*

1 Peter 5:10

Why are you so distressed in the face of this trial?
It's as if you are surprised...
   as if you think this should not be happening.[1]
My precious child, do you remember my warning?
This world is filled with troubles.
But be of good cheer,
   by my Son's sacrifice
   your troubles have all been rendered powerless
   to harm you.[2]
"Ah, but how can you say it won't harm me?" you ask.
   "I have been harmed—am being harmed—by this trial."
Dear one, take a longer view.
Examine the momentary discomfort you now suffer
   in the light of the glory that will be revealed in you.[3]

Your present suffering has a glorious purpose. It is tempering
your character so that you will fully realize the hope that is within
you.[4] Resolve to value the tempering of your character far more
than your present ease.

I do not wish you to be like others who have no hope... those
whose noteworthy character traits are written in the sand
   so that they are washed away
   with the first high tide.
I want you to be strong, firm, and steadfast in your faith.
I want you to enter my gates freely,
   to sing joyously in the presence of my Righteousness.[5]
I want to see your character honed to such a degree that
   you withstand the blaze of my Holiness
   when you enter my presence on the last day.[6]

I want you to look to the heavens in anticipation
   and not dread,
       waiting in excitement for the day
          the trumpet will sound
             and Christ will appear.[7]

[1]1 Peter 4:12; [2]John 16:33; 17:15-17; [3]Romans 8:18; [4]Romans 5:3-5; [5]Revelation 4:8-11; [6]1 Corinthians 3:12-15; [7]1 Thessalonians 4:13-18; Revelation 22:20

46 ✌ Transforming Your Life

*Make every effort to add to your faith goodness; and to
goodness, knowledge; and to knowledge, self-control; and
to self-control, perseverance; and to perseverance, godliness; and to godliness, brotherly kindness; and to brotherly
kindness, love.... For if you do these things, you will never
fall, and you will receive a rich welcome into the eternal
kingdom of our Lord and Savior Jesus Christ.*

2 Peter 1:5-7, 10-11

You yearn to know
   how to make your walk with me effective,
      how to be sure
         you will persevere in your faith
           until your very last day on earth.
You want to be sure
   that you will one day hear me say,
"Well done, good and faithful servant."[1]
Why do you fret and wonder how to accomplish these things?
I've kept no secrets from you.
My Word tells you everything you need to know about how to live
   your life in me.[2]
Of course, knowledge *about* me is not enough.
I am pleased that you seek wisdom as well as knowledge
   so that your mind will not be the only part of you
   that is transformed.
Wisdom sharpens knowledge so that it can
   penetrate your heart,
   transforming your entire life.
   Go ahead, ask me for wisdom. I delight in fulfilling my promises
to you. Wisdom will enable you to escape the temptations offered
by the world so that you may live a productive, godly life.[3]
   I equip and enable you to do my will. You do not need to groan
and strain, striving to produce good works through your own
efforts. Rather, in faith, work these things—goodness, knowledge,

self-control, perseverance, godliness, kindness, and love—into your life, massaging them into your heart and mind through constant fellowship with me, and I will one day receive you in glory, claiming you as my own.[4]

Do these things
    and wait with patient excitement
        to hear my words of affirmation on that last day.
            "Well done, good and faithful servant."

[1]Matthew 25:21, 23; [2]2 Peter 1:3; [3]2 Peter 1:4; [4]John 15:1-17

47 ✌ Dying to Self

I have been crucified with Christ and I no longer live, but
Christ lives in me.

Galatians 2:20

I know you think it's too much for me to ask... that you die to
self. But before you reject the idea, think about it. Really think
about it.

It is only in dying with Christ
that you are raised with him
... raised again to new life.
Be honest. Was your old life really so wonderful?
You have my Spirit in you now. You're set aside for righteous-
ness.[1] The lures of your old life can only make you miserable.
You think that dying to self means a life of distasteful drudgery.
Look again.
There is no drudgery in dwelling on the true,
    the noble,
        the right,
            the pure,
                everything that is worthwhile in life.[2]

There is nothing distasteful about victory; nothing repugnant
about handing all your worries to One who can actually do something about them.[3]
    Am I really asking too much when I suggest that you stop work-
ing against your new nature and cooperate with it instead?
    There is a voice in your head, even now, that clamors for atten-
tion. It's telling you that dying to self is too hard, no matter how
reasonable it may sound. That's the voice of a LIE. Don't shrink
back. Call it what it is and be done with it.
    Yes, I know it's a struggle for you sometimes. Satan's gift wrap is
often bright and cheery. It's hard not to want to open the package.

But you know from experience that his packages hold only
death,
>   destruction,
>>   and misery.[4]

Surely the package isn't *that* pretty.
I've said it before but let me say it again.
You have all that you need in order to succeed. Turn your back
on the lures of this world and die so that you can live![5]

[1]Romans 8:10-11; [2]Philippians 4:8; [3]Philippians 4:6; [4]John 10:10;
[5]Mark 8:34-36

48 ❧ Feeling Like a Failure

But the [one] who looks intently into the perfect law that gives freedom, and continues to do this, not forgetting what he had heard but doing it—he will be blessed in what he does.

James 1:25

My law bestows freedom on all who choose to live by it.
It has the power to remove
the veil of your human nature
    from the eyes of your heart
    so that you can see your own faults,
    confess them to me,
    and be utterly forgiven.[1]
My law assures freedom from the tyranny of sin and remorse
    … if you accept it.
The one who loves my Word will prosper,
    everything she undertakes will be blessed.
But the wicked will be utterly destroyed.[2]
They are lured by the saccharine words
    that come from every worldly corner.[3]
They are seduced by earthly pleasures.[4]
They pursue success as the world defines it.
Listen to my voice calling you to turn from the things of this world.
    Drink deeply of my mercy and grace through continual confession and repentance.[5]
Let others take the trophies and awards
    and all the trappings of worldly success.
Your success comes from clinging to me.
It comes from facing every challenge,
    every struggle,
    in my name and for my glory.
And it's a victory that can't decay,
    that doesn't collect dust on the mantel,

that can't be taken from you by anyone
—no matter how powerful.[6]
The battle is difficult, yes. But the reward is life itself.

[1]Romans 7:8-8:4; 1 John 1:9; [2]Psalms 1; [3]James 1:27; [4]Proverbs 21:17; [5]Proverbs 28:13; Romans 5:15-17; [6]Matthew 6:19-21

49 ᕇ Standing on the Promises

Do not be afraid. Stand firm and you will see the deliverance the Lord will bring you.... The Lord will fight for you; you need only to be still.

Exodus 14:13-14

Hemmed in on every side,
   you look for a way of escape.
Troubled and distressed,
   you search for the way to go.
Stand still instead,
   and let me prove myself your God and Savior.[1]

Fear tells you, "Give up, give in. God asks too much, expects too much. Go back to your old ways and things will be simple again."

Anger tells you, "Act now! You have rights. Don't wait for God, he's too slow. Besides, he's not the one who'll get hurt, you are!"

Pride tells you, "You can handle this. You've accomplished harder things. You can rely on all of your talents, your skills (gifts from me, remember). You don't need anyone else, not even God."

Dear one, do not listen to the voices of Fear, Anger, and Pride. Command those voices to cease.

Look to me, not only to do *something* but to do *everything*.

See the many promises I have given you... promises upon which you may safely stand?

Stand at the ready. Await further instruction with joyous anticipation. I have not failed those who came before you.[2] I will not fail you now. My unchanging love will sustain you until the day of Christ's appearing.[3]

I lead all those whom I have rescued from Satan's grasp. Rely on my strength to sustain you until the day of Christ's coming.[4]

[1]Psalm 25:4-5; 42:5; 65:5; [2]Hebrews 11:1; [3]Titus 2:11-14; [4]Exodus 15:13

50 ♆ When You're Faltering

Consider it pure joy, my brothers, whenever you face trials of many kinds, because you know that the testing of your faith develops perseverance. Perseverance must finish its work so that you may be mature and complete, not lacking anything.

James 1:2-4

Too long, you say.
This trial has besieged you for too long.
Too long according to whom?
Dear one, do you think you know what you need better than I?
Is it possible that your lack of control over this situation is what
   bothers you so? Your life will go more smoothly when you learn
   to embrace—even celebrate—your dependence on me.
I am in control.
And that is as it should be.
Celebrate the Potter's fire.
Savor the tempering of your soul.
Yes, I said "savor" it.
   The hotter the flame,
      the harder the glaze,
         the more beautiful the vessel.
You do want to be a vessel meant for noble purposes, don't you?[1]

Ask me for what you need.[2]

I never expect anything from you that I have not given you in the first place. I tell you to persevere because I have already given you the ability to do so.

My commandments are not too hard when you look to me for the strength, the patience, the courage
to perform all I expect of you.

Patiently allow the fire to finish its work. When your glaze is fully hardened you will shine with my reflected glory.[3]

[1]Romans 9:21; [2]1 John 5:14; [3]2 Corinthians 3:18

51 ∽ That It May Go Well with You

*Do what is right and good in the Lord's sight, so that it
may go well with you....*

Deuteronomy 6:18

My restrictions often chafe, rubbing you the wrong way . . . or so
it seems. My commands and stipulations often feel to you like a
too-tight garment, hemming you in, tangling around your waist.

Will you believe me when I say that they are for your good?
Taste and see that I am good.[1]

Put my commands to the test.[2]
    I have proven myself to you time and time again.[3]
        Let me prove this to you now.
I created you.
    Every hair on your head,
        every cell in your body
            is my masterpiece.

I am intimately acquainted with what makes you "tick."
I know the sort of behavior
    that will give you peace and contentment,
    a sense of well-being and joy.
You worry about the things that are
    valued by this world—
    money, status, possessions.
Fix your gaze, instead,
    on those things that are eternal.
Look to me as the source of all you need.
Set your face to seek righteousness
    —to do what is right and good in my sight—
    and I will add to your life everything else you need as well.[4]

I delight to see my children filled with joy. When I tell you that
your well-being is contingent on obeying my commands, I'm not

being manipulative or controlling, holding a club over you as a threat. I am lovingly lighting your way so that you will know the path to peace, joy, and contentment.

My Word illuminates the path; walk in it.[5]

[1]Psalms 34:8-20; 119:97-104; [2]Romans 12:1-2; [3]Deuteronomy 6:20-25; [4]Matthew 6:25-34; [5]Isaiah 30:21; John 8:12

52 ❧ Showers of Blessings

I will send down showers in season; there will be showers of blessing.

Ezekiel 34:26

Make Scripture your dwelling place
    in both the wet and the dry seasons of the soul
    so that you may enjoy my grace and mercy
    all of your days,
    regardless of your circumstances.
Turn your face toward me,
    because only I command the skies.
I open the doors of heaven
    to pour out all you need.[1]
Make love and truth your companions.
Knit them into the fabric of your life
    and write them on your heart.
Let my showers of blessing
    paint your soul a lush green.
Then you will find favor and honor with me
    and with all people everywhere.[2]
I will shield you from the scorching heat
    and freely give you a bounty of good things.[3]
Do not let your circumstances
    dictate your frame of mind.
Whether you are experiencing a season of drought or abundance,
I have set you aside for myself and made you holy.[4]
Look to me.
I will make your land rich in every way
    and give you strength enough to see you through
    to the very end.
I will sustain you so that your land will be filled with blessings until
the day of Jesus Christ.[5]

‡Psalms 78:23; Philippians 1:19; ²Proverbs 3:3-4; ³Psalms 84:11; 1 John 4:18; ⁴1 Corinthians 1:2; 1 Peter 2:9; ⁵1 Corinthians 1:4-9

53 ॐ When You're Afraid of Satan

You, dear children, are from God and have overcome them, because the one who is in you is greater than the one who is in the world.

1 John 4:4

Don't be afraid, my little one; you do not face your troubles alone. It is true that this world is full of troubling events and ideologies, but my son, Jesus Christ, has vanquished your Enemy once and for all.[1]

Lately you have surrendered your focus on my provision and promises and focused, instead, on Satan's evil. Precious child, I have *all* power. Cease anxiously searching the sky for signs of Satan's evil schemes against you and look for *my* hand in all of your circumstances. True, Satan may be the instigator of some of your circumstances, but he must always respect the limits I set for him.[2]

As you realign your focus, learning to see even your trials as my perfect will for your life, do not lose hope, thinking, "This means my Father does not love me. He has abandoned me or perhaps he has something against me."[3] Remember that my purpose is always your ultimate good. I use Satan's opposition to *bless* you. I allow obstacles to overtake you to help you become more mature, to assist you to grow strong in your faith and discipline, to make you a steadfast example for others.

Trials offer opportunities to exalt me despite danger and persecution... chances to make choices that glorify me and point the way for others to follow. Your unwavering faith as you endure hardships today may provide the encouragement necessary for another to persist courageously tomorrow, and it will surely give the angels reason to rejoice.[4]

Be careful to resist the temptation to fall back on your own devices in your desire to oppose Satan's craftiness. Teeth-gritting perseverance will not see you through to the end. Your own cleverness, energy, and stamina are not adequate grounds on which to take a stand in defense of a relationship... a ministry... a life. But do not be discouraged. Lean on me. Rely on my strength. Draw on my power.[5] My Holy Spirit within you is far more powerful than Satan and his demons.

Submission to me makes all things bearable. Maturity in the Christian walk is, quite simply, the desire to praise and glorify me regardless of your circumstances. When your desire is to glorify me, then even death is gain.[6]

[1]John 16:33: Philippians 2:6-11; 1 John 4:2; [2]Job 1:6-12; 2:1-7; [3]Exodus 17:7; [4]2 Corinthians 1:3-4; 7:4-16; Philippians 1:14; Colossians 1:24-2:5; 1 Thessalonians 3:7; [5]Ephesians 6:10-20; [6]Philippians 1:18-21

54 ✦ Painful Lessons

He who began a good work in you will carry it on to completion until the day of Christ Jesus.

Philippians 1:6

I hear your cry, my lovely one.[1]
Do not be discouraged.
I am your loving Father
    even when you make mistakes.[2]
Even your mistakes were visible to me
    before I set the earth upon its foundation[3]
    … and still I loved you before you ever came to be.

You sometimes see yourself as a "hopeless case." I am pleased by your desire to obey me, my child, but you should know that I do not see you as hopeless—even when you make mistakes. I see you clothed in the white robes of righteousness, a recipient of my grace, which I've lavished on you.[4]

You want to rush headlong into a state of holiness, while I want you to learn the valuable lessons I've set for you along the way. Trust me. Trust that I, who have called you by name and claimed you for my own,[5] will thoroughly purify you as well.[6]

I have called you, not so that you may be a perfect witness, entirely holy in yourself—for that is impossible—but so that you may stand as a testimony to *my* purpose and grace in your life.[7]

Trust me. When things don't go as you hope, trust me. When you do not seem to be growing as you think you should, trust me. When you make a mistake, trust me to teach you the lessons you need to learn from that mistake and—in partnership with my Holy Spirit—endeavor to learn them. Trust me to work in you in accordance with my plans and purpose for you.[8]

My work in you will be completed on the day my Son returns to meet you in the air. Be patient and cheerful, knowing that you are justified—and being sanctified—from now until the trumpet sounds.[9]

[1]Jeremiah 29:11-14; [2]Joshua 31:8; [3]Psalms 102:25-28; [4]Philippians 1:7; Ephesians 1:7-8; [5]2 Thessalonians 2:13-16; [6]1 Thessalonians 5:24; [7]2 Timothy 1:8-10; [8]Philippians 2:13; [9]1 Thessalonians 4:16-17

55 ৯ Out of My Glorious Riches

Now to him who is able to do immeasurably more than all
we ask or imagine, according to his power that is at work
within us, to him be glory in the church and in Christ
Jesus throughout all generations, for ever and ever!
Ephesians 3:20-21

You are dissatisfied with the life you lead; you desire a deeper relationship with me. You want more from your life. It delights me to
see such desires come to full bloom. I will always satisfy them.[1]

You are part of my family line. I gave you my name, and like any
good Father, I intend to train you to live according to your heritage.[2] Through diligent instruction and loving prayers (yours and
others') I will expose the strength and power you received when
you were born (again).[3]

I know that you often regard my instruction as difficult. There
are times when you wish you didn't have such an unrelenting
Father. But, dear one, I want only what is best for you. I want you
to fully comprehend the depth of my love for you and to be filled
to overflowing with my Spirit.[4]

So go on wrestling with your human nature. Call out my name.
Shout for my help! I never grow weary of hearing your voice; never
tire of answering your prayers. Don't assume that your human
nature is an obstacle to your prayers, rather, pray all the more.
Wrestle with me as Jacob, the "Sly One," did![5] He received the
name Israel, "God-fighter," in return for his night's labor. If your
human nature has named you "Deceiver," ask me to change your
name to "Trustworthy"; if "Despair," cry out to me to deliver you
and proclaim you "Joy"; if "Gossip," ask my help and receive the
name "Discreet"; if "Lazy," ask me to rename you "Industrious." I
will do it just as I did for Jacob, but it will take a restructuring of
your nature. Jacob wrestled with me and won a new name at the
cost of a life-long limp. Your human nature will have to die so that
godliness may live in you, but the prize is of greater worth than
gold... I promise you.[6]

Go ahead, ask me for what you need. Say it! Say, "I will not let you go until you bless me!"

[1]Psalms 103:5; [2]Psalms 119:105-112; [3]Ephesians 3:14-16; [4]Ephesians 3:17-19; [5]Genesis 32:22-31; [6]Romans 6

56 ∾ Springs of Joy

*Do not be conformed to this world but be transformed by
the renewing of your mind, that you may prove what the
will of God is, that which is good and acceptable and perfect.*

Romans 12:2, NASB

When you feel at odds with yourself,
> come to me.

When relationships break down,
> come to me.

When life doesn't seem to fit
> and you squirm in your skin
> as if it were two sizes too small,
>> come to me
> and I will give you peace.[1]

The world tells you to seek comfort in people and things at
times such as these. Worldly advisors whisper life-strangling mes-
sages in your ear, telling you to "stand up for your rights."

They tell you to "expand" your consciousness and make life fit
more comfortably by turning your back on loved ones, friends who
fail you, brothers and sisters in the Lord who don't meet your
expectations.

Such actions only diminish you. The end result is a shriveled,
undernourished soul.

How can that expand your life?

When you squirm in your skin, when relationships are fractured,
when you're feeling out of joint, kneel at the Cross. At the Cross
relationships are restored, divisions are mended, one's soul is
stretched to fit.

Speak blessings to those who hurt you.[2] Model yourself after
your brother, Jesus, praying for those who mistreat you, so that you
may receive a reward.[3]

Put me to the test. Let me prove to you how good and pleasing it is to live according to my instruction.

Place your trust in me. I want to revive your soul and make you wise. I want to fill you with peace and joy.

True joy springs from obedience alone.

Let me give you a joyful heart.

[1]Matthew 11:28-30; [2]Romans 12:14; [3]Matthew 5:43-48; [4]Psalms 19:7-13

57 ❧ In Times of Trial

*And we rejoice in the hope of the glory of God. Not only so,
but we also rejoice in our sufferings, because we know that
suffering produces perseverance; perseverance, character;
and character, hope.*

Romans 5:2-4

Take that which is plaguing you today, my child, and place it in my
hands. Do you feel the warmth of my hand as you pass your worries
to me? I am living, vibrant, and powerful.[1]

I love you, my child.
I love you more than you can possibly imagine,
and I am completely devoted to your good.

It pleases me when you nestle in my protective embrace and
trust me even when you're suffering.

I am confident that you can persevere through this trial. I know,
because I was the one who gave you perseverance.

Don't you see?

The outcome is fixed.

I have already arranged for you to win. I knew—from the beginning of time—every trial you would ever face. I gave you the exact
qualities and gifts you need in order to succeed. You may draw on
them any time you wish.

I do not discipline as earthly fathers do. They sometimes discipline their children mistakenly, according to their own whim.

You can be absolutely sure that all of my lessons, even the lessons
that only suffering can teach, are for *your* good.

My lessons produce righteousness and peace in all who submit
to them.[2]

Trials purge and purify your faith, proving it to be genuine.

Your faith is worth even more than gold.

Gold is purified by fire, but one day it will perish, consumed by
the fires of Judgment.

Genuine faith is incombustible.

I do not wish to see you shamed by lack of preparation.

Trials overtake you in order to transform your very character so that you will be prepared to meet your future. And a transformation of character brings with it hope—hope for the future. With such hope you can meet any test the Evil One may send your way.

This is your hope: Your faith, having been purified by trials, will pass through the fire and will be cause for praise, glory, and honor when Jesus Christ is revealed on the Last Day.[3]

[1]Revelation 1:14-18; [2]Hebrews 12:10-11; [3]1 Peter 1:7

58 ᔗ Needing Comfort

Praise be to the God and Father of our Lord Jesus Christ,
the Father of compassion and the God of all comfort, who
comforts us in all our troubles, so that we can comfort
those in any trouble with the comfort we ourselves have
received from God.

2 Corinthians 1:3-4

Child of mine, loved and cherished one, your burden is great and it grows heavier with each fearful question. "Why would One who is sovereign allow such suffering?" "Has God stopped loving me? Did he ever love me? Have I been fooling myself?" Do not fear, my beloved. I have not abandoned you. Even in your pain, I hold you close; I cradle you against my chest, as a mother with her infant.[1]

Ah, you see? The vise-grip on your heart is loosening already. It is good to be reminded that you are not alone.

Let suffering do its work. Let it teach you to rely on me and not yourself.[2] Your tears water your relationship with me, encouraging you to grow toward the Light, helping your roots sink deep into the joys of life and the priceless pleasures of my eternal presence.[3]

When you are delivered from your troubles you will sing praise songs to me and many will hear what I have done for you— how I delivered you from sorrow and comforted every heartache. Because of your testimony, they will stand in awe before me and place their trust in me.[4]

Nevermore will others be forced to say, "I looked for sympathy, but there was none; for comforters, but I found none."[5] You will share your comfort and enjoy a new sense of purpose. You will weep with those who weep because you know how they feel.[6] You will embrace them with strong arms because you once had empty arms. You will be equipped to be my emissary, to be a shining example in others' lives, crowning them with beauty and joy where there was mourning and despair.[7] You will harvest the seeds of comfort, joy, and contentment I have sown in your life and plant them in others' lives. Your crops will multiply and—no matter how much you give—you will gather far greater joy, bask in still deeper comfort, know even more contentment. And one day, in the not too distant future, you will enter my presence with singing and you will wear a crown of joy forevermore.[8]

[1]Isaiah 66:13; [2]2 Corinthians 1:8-9; [3]Psalms 16:11; [4]Psalms 40:3; [5]Psalms 69:20; [6]Romans 12:15; [7]Isaiah 61:3; [8]Psalms 126:5; Isaiah 51:11

59 ✍ Discipline

No discipline seems pleasant at the time, but painful.
Later on, however, it produces a harvest of righteousness
and peace for those who have been trained by it.

Hebrews 12:11

I know how hard my lessons can seem at times. In fact, there are
   times, I know, when you think that I have made the entire world
   into one huge, uncomfortable classroom…
   and you long for summer vacation.
But today you have made me a proud Father
   because you have sought me in the midst of this
   painful lesson.
Hold tight to me, my lovely child,
   and rest in the assurance that *my* plans
   are best for you.
I, who set the boundaries of the sea,
   have set the boundaries of your life.
Schoolyard bullies may shout and intimidate
   but they cannot triumph against you.[1]
         I will not let you perish amid the crowd.
            I will reach down and draw you out of the mob.[2]
               I will lift you when you fall.
                  I will shelter you beneath my wing.[3]

My plans for you are for your good.[4]
Nothing can ever happen to you over which I do not have control.
So trust me, my child.
Trust that I do not discipline according to human whim.
I discipline for your sake.[5]
Trust that I love you enough
   to mold you into the image of my precious Son.
So lift up your head and face this lesson squarely.
Stand straight and tall in the middle of this schoolyard
   where I've placed you for a time.

Continue to endure with patience,
  refusing to give up,
so that when the lesson ends
  you will receive righteousness and peace.[6]

[1]Jeremiah 5:22; [2]Psalms 18:16; [3]Psalms 91; [4]Jeremiah 29:11-13;
[5]Hebrews 12; [6]Galatians 6:9

60 ✌ A Way of Escape

No temptation has seized you except what is common to man. And God is faithful; he will not let you be tempted beyond what you can bear. But when you are tempted, he will also provide a way out so that you can stand up under it.

1 Corinthians 10:13

You find yourself on a steep and rocky path,
　　blind curves and sheer cliffs on every side.
You are tempted to despair, but
　　be at peace, my little one.
This path is unfamiliar to you, it's true,
　　but not to me.
I always knew I would lead you on this path one day.
I have chosen this particular path
　　through this specific trial
　　especially for you,
　　and it will serve to perfect you...
　　if you trust me.
You'll see.

But first...
　　Do you recall that even in the midst of the most difficult tempta-tion my grace is ample? Do you remember that it is my power and not your own that has brought you through other such tests? It will be my power once again, I promise you, because my power is dis-played to perfection through your weakness.[1]
　　You have never been assailed by any temptation that proved to be too much for you when you placed your trust in me... never...[2]
　　nor will you.
I have already provided a way out.
　　In the meantime, keep in mind that grumbling is seductive and it betrays a dangerous lack of trust in me. You can trust me to see you through to the end of this trial. If you do not trust me, you will

be tempted to trust yourself.

You see now what I mean by "dangerous," don't you? You need have no fear as long as you understand that I am in control, for I am faithful.[3] If you trust to your own devices, you have every reason to be afraid.

You are right to treat temptation with respect. It is always best to understand your limitations. Only a fool tries to see how close she can venture to the flame.

But I *have* no limits.

My power cannot be overcome![4]

I have used my power to create a way of escape.

So do not try to stand your ground in the face of this—or any—temptation.

Take the way I have provided you.

Fly!

[1]2 Corinthians 12:9; [2]Psalms 28:7; Romans 9:33; [3]Deuteronomy 32:3-4; [4]2 Chronicles 20:6-9

61 ∻ When You Grow Weary in Well-Doing

Thanks be to God! He gives us the victory through our Lord Jesus Christ. Therefore, my dear [sisters], stand firm. Let nothing move you. Always give yourselves fully to the work of the Lord, because you know that your labor in the Lord is not in vain.

1 Corinthians 15:57-58

Your energy is flagging. Your eyes have slipped to focus on your feet instead of the goal ahead. You move more slowly with every step. Look up, my weary one. Lift up your downcast heart and be of good cheer.[1] Your labor and the love you continually display toward my children have not gone unnoticed.[2]

Your service pleases me very much but you are so busy doing for others you have forgotten to ask on your own behalf. I grant the heart's desires of all who delight in Christ-like acts of loving-kindness; they are honored and not shamed.[3] Ask for whatever you will and I will give it to you.[4] If you need strength, ask and it is yours. If you need endurance and perseverance, ask and you will have them. Ask and I will make a way through the pressing urgency of your many tasks so that you will enjoy rest and contentment as you do them.[5]

I will see that you behold the fruit of your labor. You will rejoice with me for all of my children whose lives you touch and I will beam with pride over you, my child. I will give you joy in the daytime and touch your racing thoughts so that you can sleep in peace.[6]

Cease striving and meditate on who I am.[7] When you do, your thoughts will be calm and you will accomplish more than you ever dreamed.

Take heart, my obedient child. Fix your eyes on the prize—the victory that is yours in Jesus Christ. Know that you run this race, not for an earthly prize that will pass away, but for a crown that will outlast time itself.[8]

[1]Psalms 145:14; [2]Hebrews 6:10; [3]John 12:26; Psalms 37:4; Joel 2:26; [4]James 5:16; 1 John 3:22; [5]John 16:23-24; Matthew 21:22; Mark 11:24; [6]Psalms 4:8; [7]Psalms 46:10; [8]1 Corinthians 9:24-27; James 1:12

62 ❧ The Beginning of Wisdom

The fear of the Lord is the beginning of wisdom; all who follow his precepts have good understanding.

Psalms 111:10

Fear has recently become a dirty word. It did not used to be so. There was a time when good people acknowledged that some fears were healthy... demonstrating wisdom. That is the kind of wisdom I desire to place in your heart. I am not bound by fads. I do not rewrite my Word or change my message based on the latest popular psychological mumblings... or rantings.

A fool is still a fool, regardless of the name you call him. A fool is one who claims wisdom in the absence of a clear understanding of my Word; one who makes judgments based on a standard other than my own.

Fear has been judged by fools. Slavish followers of popular theory speak of it only in hushed, shameful tones. The very idea of fear has been all but banished from polite conversation.

My precious one, listen to me! Fear can be a life-saver! When you were a child it was fear that prevented you from dashing into the roadway, it was fear that snatched your hand back from a flame. Fear is only bad when it's unfounded. I love you too much to teach you to be absurdly brave. I established my precepts for your protection and there are consequences to ignoring them.

A foolish person allows every passing fad to tickle her ears, turning her face into each fickle wind as it blows past. She builds her house upon sand.[1] A wise person loves my law![2] She listens intently for my voice,[3] turning her face to me.[4] She builds her house upon the Rock.[5]

I am holy and absolutely righteous.[6] Your holy reverence for me demonstrates an understanding of who I AM.[7]

Only a fool believes that my standards are not perfect and completely unforgiving. But *I am* forgiving. I have fulfilled the promise I made in ages past. I have made you clean, your sins no longer condemn you.[8] They are washed white as snow.[9]

135

I sent my Son, not to condemn but to save. I sent him to bind up the brokenhearted, to shout "Freedom!" to those in bondage and release them from the imprisoning forces of their sinful nature. I want to pour out gladness over every moment of your life. Instead of shame, I grant forgiveness; and where there was disgrace, joy. All who are wise are clothed for all eternity in a garment of salvation and my Son's robe of righteousness.[10]

[1]Matthew 7:24-27; [2]Psalms 119; [3]Deuteronomy 30:19, 20; 1 Samuel 13:22; [4]Psalms 27:7-13; [5]Deuteronomy 32:1-6; Psalms 92:15; [6]Isaiah 6:1-8; [7]Exodus 3:13-14; [8]Romans 8; [9]Psalms 51; [10]Isaiah 61

63 ᎌ Creeping Dissatisfaction

*Let them give thanks to the Lord for his unfailing love
and his wonderful deeds for men, for he satisfies the thirsty
and fills the hungry with good things.*

Psalm 107:8-9

Your patience grows thin.

Irritation pokes through your veil of concentration as you perform every daily task.

You regard each menial duty as make-work preventing you from
moving into your "true calling."

Like a well-trained racehorse
    straining at his reins and pawing the dirt,
        you are eager to get on with your "race."

You acknowledge my sovereignty in the major events and circumstances of your life but forget that *all* of creation rests within
the borders of my hand. You overlook the fact that the tiniest creatures exist as much according to the order I have established as do
the planets and solar systems. I have infused the spirit of order into
my universe. At my bidding, locusts march together in ranks.[1]

I have not overlooked your many talents.

Menial tasks are as much a part of my plan for your life as "glorious" ones. Lowly chores, cheerfully completed in my name, please
me just as much as glorious offerings.

Each duty is beautiful in its season
    and public performance
        at the price of personal holiness
           is no offering at all.

I consider every effort you make to be at peace with your brothers and sisters and to nurture unity among them to be the noblest

of offerings—no matter how "menial" or "insignificant."[2]

Wait patiently even as my own Son waited patiently for his time to come.[3] Be proud to consider yourself a servant on the same order as Jesus Christ.[4] Then I will fulfill the longing of your soul.[5]

You were united with Christ when your old nature was put to death along with him. Now your new nature lives in and through your risen Savior. So count yourself dead to the sins of impatience and irritation (which are simply other names for a lack of trust in my sovereignty).[6] Rather, offer yourself to me as a living sacrifice.[7]

When dissatisfaction creeps in, remember that the world's standards are not my standards.[8] It pleases me when my children choose to be last and trust me to make them first... in my time.[9]

[1]Proverbs 30:25-28; [2]Ephesians 4:1-7; [3]John 13:1; Acts 15:18; [4]Galatians 4:4; John 13:1-17; [5]Psalms 107:4-16; Luke 9:48; [6]Romans 6:5-14; [7]Romans 12:1-2; [8]Isaiah 55:8-9; [9]Matthew 19:28-30; 20:16, 25-28

64 ‿ Reviving the Soul

The law of the Lord is perfect, reviving the soul. The statutes of the Lord are trustworthy, making wise the simple. The precepts of the Lord are right, giving joy to the heart. The commands of the Lord are radiant, giving light to the eyes. The fear of the Lord is pure, enduring forever. The ordinances of the Lord are sure and altogether righteous. They are more precious than gold, than much pure gold; they are sweeter than honey, than honey from the comb. By them is your servant warned; in keeping them is great reward.

Psalms 19:7-11

When you believe that my promises will be accomplished and you obey my commands, you will be blessed with good things.[1]

Wherever you go,
   whatever you do,
      you will prosper.[2]

Your path will be straight and wide as a sunbeam.[3]
You will remain constantly in my presence and
I will bring you honor.[4]
You will speak truth and
   be known for your wisdom.
I will pour mercy on your head
   and it will flow over you, soothing your soul.[5]

I will attend to your prayers as you feast upon my Word and obey
   it.[6] You will know who you are, know where you are going.[7]
You will dwell in peace because you are calmly secure in my love.[8]
You will sink your roots deep, like a tree planted by a stream.
Your life will be fruitful, and your family, blessed.[9]
You will be virtuous, strong, patient, and joyful.[10]
Your beauty will put the sun and stars to shame.[11]

The words of your mouth and the works of your hands will be a constant testimony to others, bringing glory to me.[12]

Great will be your reward in heaven.[13]

[1]Luke 1:45; [2]1 Kings 2:3; [3]Proverbs 4:18; [4]John 12:26; [5]Psalms 23:5-6; [6]1 John 3:22; James 5:16; [7]Ephesians 1:4-5; John 14:1-3; [8]Philippians 4:9; Ephesians 3:14-19; [9]Psalms 1:1-3; Proverbs 31:23, 28; [10]Colossians 1:10-11; [11]Daniel 12:3; [12]Matthew 5:16; [13]Matthew 5:19

65 ॐ The Advantage of Confession

*You are my hiding place; you will protect me from trouble
and surround me with songs of deliverance.*

Psalms 32:7

When you truly believe that I am a forgiving God; when you honestly trust that my Son paid the entire price for your redemption, then you will no longer fear confession.[1] You will perceive the privilege it is to come into my presence with a repentant heart, to be washed clean.[2] You will grasp the joy and gratitude that activate obedience in my children.[3] You will understand that I am not only willing but *delighted* to forgive those whom I have chosen to be my children

> ... and all the benefits of a clean heart
> will be yours.

Those with unclean hearts groan from the weight of their guilt. Their sins are parasites, eating away body and soul. Their energy is sapped as if by the scorching heat of an oppressive summer's day. Those who are forgiven, whose hearts are pure in my sight, receive blessings without number.[4]

My children repent and pray so they may be restored to full fellowship.

They know there is safety in my presence.

They trust me to be their hiding place... to keep them free from harm.

They know I surround them with angels to guard and protect them... angels singing songs of victory because the battle is already won.[5]

Come, live in safety and be at ease.[6] Trust yourself to my unfailing love.[7] Trust me to forgive you freely when you come to me with a broken **and** contrite heart. Come! Be cleansed and healed.

[1]Nehemiah 9:17; Psalms 103:1-4; Daniel 9:9; Mark 11:25; Colossians 1:13-14; 3:13; 1 John 1:9; Acts 13:38-39; 26:15-18; [2]Hebrews 10:19-24; Revelation 7:13-17; [3]Psalms 31:7-8; 68:3-5; Acts 2:25-28, 46; 1 Corinthians 15:57; 2 Corinthians 2:14; Colossians 3:15-17; Hebrews 12:28; [4]Psalms 32:1-4; [5]2 Kings 6:15-17; Psalms 40:3; 91; 96; 98; 100; [6]Proverbs 1:33; [7]Psalms 32:10

66 ⌘ Impatient with God's Plan

Therefore we also, since we are surrounded by so great a cloud of witnesses, let us lay aside every weight, and the sin which so easily ensnares us, and let us run with endurance the race that is set before us, looking unto Jesus, the author and finisher of our faith, who for the joy that was set before him endured the cross, despising the shame, and has sat down at the right hand of the throne of God.

Hebrews 12:1-2, NKJV

Dear one, you grow anxious unnecessarily. I have everything under control. If you settle calmly into my plan and accept my timetable for your life, you will enjoy the journey more. I fulfill my promises—every one of them—at the proper time.[1] Your doubts are born of a foreshortened view of time.

From the beginning it was my plan to redeem your race through my Son,[2] yet many of my people died in faith, still looking toward the hope that was, for them, in the distant future.[3] And because I kept my full plan a mystery until the time it was fulfilled, many had far less upon which to base their hope than you do from your vantage point in history.[4] You already possess your greatest hope and reward. My promise is fulfilled in you.[5]

Practice patience, my child. Believe that I am faithful; I do not delay. At the proper time I will satisfy both your needs and desires.[6] Jacob wrestled through the night before his prayer was answered.[7] My servant, Paul, asked three times to have his thorn removed, but my plan was a better one and my grace was sufficient to sustain him.[8] His patience caused him to grow in faith and provided opportunities for him to testify to my love and mercy toward him.

Rest in my arms. Drink in the teaching of my Word while I work out my perfect will for your sake. Shelter in the shade of my grace—it is a haven of rest and safety—while you continue to pray earnestly and with fervor because that, too, will be used for your benefit. Your prayers draw you into my presence; abiding in my presence equips and matures you in ways you cannot even imagine now.

Christ Jesus, the one who began the work of faith within you, will finish it to perfection. So walk in faith, not according to what you see.[9] Choose that same path of faith as those other shining examples chose so long ago.[10] They have run this race before you and have been declared victors by virtue of their faith. They stand at the sidelines even now, cheering you on toward the finish line.

[1]Genesis 21:2; [2]Genesis 3:15; [3]Hebrews 11:13; [4]Ephesians 3:1-6; [5]Colossians 1:27; [6]Psalms 145:15-16; [7]Genesis 32:24; [8]2 Corinthians 12:7-10; [9]Philippians 1:6; [10]Hebrews 11

PART FOUR

જી

God's Promise to Encourage Us

67 ✧ Waiting on God

If we are faithless, he (Christ) will remain faithful, for he cannot disown himself.

2 Timothy 2:13

Why do you fret, my little one? Why weep?
I called you to myself
    before I formed the earth
    and set it spinning through space.
Before I ever taught the sun
    where to rise and set,
    I had you in mind.[1]
All of creation testifies to my magnificent power
    and divine nature.[2]
Even so, creation itself will wear out
    like a beloved and much-worn garment;
    I will roll it up like a comfortable old bathrobe,
    but I will remain...
    and you will remain with me.[3]
There will come a day when I will change creation
    with the ease with which you change your clothes.
But I will remain the same for all eternity.[4]

So continue praying, don't fret because I have not yet answered.
    Watch patiently and gratefully for the answers to your prayers because I am faithful.[5]
    Trust in me.
    Dwell serenely in a hopeful state of faith.
    True faith doesn't die when answers are not immediate. Trust that this delay serves my purpose, I have not overlooked you, I have only your ultimate good in mind.
    You have entrusted your requests—your needs—to me. Be convinced now, that I am able to guard your heart and mind against the schemes of the Evil One right up to the day you come to reign with me forever.[6]

Adopt an eternal perspective and keep praying! I long to be gracious to you, to demonstrate my compassion in your life. I will be gracious when you cry for help. I will answer you and show you the way you should go.[7]

Wait patiently in the shelter of my wings and you will receive all I have promised.[8]

[1]Psalms 136; Ephesians 1:3-12; [2]Romans 1:20; [3]Revelation 7:9-17; [4]Hebrews 1:10-12; [5]Colossians 4:2; [6]2 Timothy 1:12; [7]Isaiah 30:18-21; [8] Psalms 61:1-4; Hebrews 6:13-15

68 ॐ Moving Mountains

I tell you the truth, if you have faith as small as a mustard seed, you can say to this mountain, "Move from here to there" and it will move. Nothing will be impossible for you.

Matthew 17:20

I chose you to be my child before time began.
With joy I called you from the fruitless,
    dead-end existence of sinners
    which was once yours,
    to be holy and blameless.[1]
I made you a priest
able to offer spiritual sacrifices to me
    through prayer.[2]
I made you a partner with my Holy Spirit to serve me
    in praise and thanksgiving.[3]
To me, your prayers are golden bowls
    of sweet-smelling incense.[4]

Don't say your faith is too puny to partner with me. My Holy Spirit will assist you in your weakness. When you don't know how to pray, he does. My Spirit will intercede for you, weaving the sweet sounds of your prayers with my purposes, harmonizing your expectant petitions with my will.[5]

It is only to those who lack faith
    that my promise to honor a mountain-moving request
    has become merely a figure of speech.
To those who demonstrate my righteousness in their lives,
    all things are possible
    because the heartfelt prayer of a righteous person
    is powerful and effective.[6]

Believe that I...
>the God who hung each star in its place
>and calls it by its own name...
>the God who set the planets in their orbits
>and laid the footings for earth's foundation...
>I will answer even your most daring requests,
>when you ask according to my will.[7]

[1]Ephesians 1:4-5; 2:1-10; [2]1 Peter 2:4-9; [3]1 Corinthians 3:9; Revelation 1:5-6; [4]Revelation 5:8; 8:1-5; [5]Romans 8:26-27; [6]Matthew 19:26; James 5:16; [7]Isaiah 40:26; 1 John 5:14-15

69 ✣ Throwing Off the Chains of Guilt

Here is a trustworthy saying that deserves full acceptance:
Christ Jesus came into the world to save sinners—of which
I am the worst. But for that very reason I was shown
mercy so that in me, the worst of sinners, Christ Jesus
might display his unlimited patience as an example for
those who would believe on him and receive eternal life.

1 Timothy 1:15-16

You think your sins are too big
  —too black a blot—
  for my grace and mercy to erase.
You look at the ticking clock of your life
  and tell yourself,
    "It is too late now to call God's name,
    he will not listen."
Not so, my child!
My ears are attuned to your voice. I will hear your cry
  above the din of all the world.
When you seek me you will find me.[1] My servant, Paul, sought to
  serve me in the most heinous way, by persecuting my Church.
  Yet I heard even his outraged cry and I arranged for him to find
  me on the road to Damascus. I will do as much for you, my anxious child.
Do not fear.[2] Do not throw up your hands
  and throw open the door to discouragement,
  allowing it to settle into your heart.
I am your all-powerful God and I have pledged myself to you.
I not only sustain you, I pardon you for all time.[3] I have declared
  that Satan's pronouncement—"Guilty as charged!"—is null and
  void.[4]
Call out my name. Let me make an example of you... an example
  of my unlimited patience, love, and mercy.

My love is rock solid
  and more enduring than granite.
      Let me hide you in the cleft of the Rock.[5]

[1]Jeremiah 29:11-13; [2]Zechariah 8:13; [3]Isaiah 41:10; [4]Colossians 9:14; [5]Psalms 18:2

70 ♪ No Longer Alone

You are no longer foreigners and aliens, but fellow citizens with God's people and members of God's household, built on the foundation of the apostles and prophets, with Christ Jesus himself as the chief cornerstone.

Ephesians 2:19-20

You've spent your life feeling alone and out of step; feeling like a stranger, like you don't belong. You're home now. Come, climb into my lap. Let me croon songs of welcome in your ear.

Rest for a while in my embrace. Let me softly brush the troubling thoughts from your mind and give you tranquility.[1]

You will never be alone again.
I am always with you.
Never again will you be fatherless, homeless, hopeless.
I am your loving Father.
Your home is with me.
Your hope is in me.
Your new home is of the sturdiest material.
Every stone of the foundation has been fired in the searing flames
  of suffering and pain...[2]
  chiseled by the double-edged sword of my Word...[3]
  fitted into place by my incomparable hand.
The Cornerstone is perfectly suited.
It has been tested and proved able
  —having borne the weight of all the sins of the world—
      to support and define the entire structure,
            which is my Church.

And, having been properly fitted into the structure yourself, you have been called to share in the joys and responsibilities of living as a part of it—my family of believers.[4]

From the day I rescued you and your citizenship was transferred to my heavenly city,[5] you have had a place with me; a place where no other can fit; a place reserved for you and you alone since before the world began.

You have come home. No longer will you wander as an alien. Take your proper place as a child of the king.[6]

[1]Isaiah 26:3; [2]Hebrews 11; [3]Hebrews 4:12; [4]Galatians 6:10; [5]Hebrews 12:22-24; [6]1 John 3:1

71 ৯ When You Feel Betrayed

"Because he loves me," says the Lord, "I will rescue him; I will protect him, for he acknowledges my name. He will call upon me, and I will answer him; I will be with him in trouble, I will deliver him and honor him."

Psalms 91:14-15

There are few injuries as hurtful as betrayal. I know, because my Son experienced betrayal of the most treacherous kind.[1] You are not alone in this, despite the way you feel. I am with you, even in this present trouble.[2]

I am not blind to your pain; your pain penetrates to the very core of your being. It flows through your thoughts, blurring your vision. You search your heart for a cause, you gaze through tears at the ruins of your relationship. You feel as if emptiness stalks you in your waking hours and mocks you when you close your eyes to rest. And you wonder why I tarry.

Trust me, dear child, and practice contentment despite your present circumstances.[3] The hole in your heart isn't a mortal wound. In fact, far from being deadly, it has the potential to rekindle within your heart a determination to live in and for me and me alone. It serves to remind you that your relationship with me is the only certainty in all the world.[4]

In an attitude of forgiveness, struggle with the challenge of this broken relationship, refusing to yield to the temptation to retaliate, to seek vengeance.[5] Contend with it in such a way that you remind others of Christ's example.[6] Show others how to dress their wounds and continue to struggle with their sinful tendencies, despite them.[7] And when victory becomes a fact, instead of a well-worn dream, all of heaven will sing in celebration.

The lure of human relationships is so great that this is one of my most often repeated lessons. Let me gently remind you to keep your eyes fixed on me rather than gazing upon the charred and broken pieces of this relationship.[8] You will rise from the ashes, a more tempered vessel. I will deliver you and bring you honor and you will commit yourself, all the more, to abiding only in me.

[1]Matthew 26:21-26; 1 Peter 4:13; [2]Isaiah 41:10; Psalms 91:1-2; [3]Philippians 4:10-13; [4]John 15; Deuteronomy 4:31; 31:6; [5]Romans 12:19; Ephesians 4:31-32; [6]1 Peter 2:21-24; [7]Romans 8:1-17; [8]Hebrews 12:1-13

72 ॐ Seeking Contentment

I have learned to be content whatever the circumstances...
I have learned the secret of being content in any and every
situation, whether well fed or hungry, whether living in
plenty or in want. I can do everything through him who
gives me strength.

Philippians 4:13

Discontent is a common human trait, but never mind, I have the
answer for you. You are growing tired of doing what is right simply
for the sake of obedience. You see others—who are not obedient—
flourishing, and you wonder at times when you will see some
reward for your labor.[1]

Some who claim my name even picture
    lands and possessions
        and wonder when theirs will be arriving,
            as if their salvation were a ticket
                on a ride to
                    "Happiness."
I'm glad that you seek to be content, my precious one.
I have a higher purpose planned for your life
    than you can possibly imagine.[2]
So joyfully do what is right,
    knowing as you do
    that you are not on a ride to happiness;
    you are on a pilgrimage toward holiness.[3]
I do not merely want you to be fulfilled;
    I want you to be transformed![4]
Having been justified through my son, Jesus Christ,
    I want you to be transformed from your present glory
    —which is considerable—
    into a mirror image
    of his glory which is yet to be fully revealed.[5]

It's true that a person reaps what she sows, but the harvest of obedience is so much greater than happy circumstances and simple material possessions.

Be of good cheer, my child, you have already received the greatest rewards of all—and those, for free! From me you have received eternal life and you have been sealed with my Holy Spirit who strengthens, equips, and empowers you, making you equal to any challenge, any circumstance.[6]

So be content and wait upon me as I complete my masterpiece... which is your life, lived for me.[7]

[1]Psalms 73; [2]Romans 5:1-2; Ephesians 3:20; [3]Colossians 1:22-23; [4]Romans 12:1-2; [5]1 John 3:2; [6]Galatians 6:8-10; Ephesians 1:13-14; [7]Ephesians 2:10; Philippians 1:3-6; 2:12-13; 2 Timothy 3:16-17

73 ॐ In Times of Desperation

The Lord is near to all who call on him, to all who call on him in truth. He fulfills the desires of those who fear him; he hears their cry and saves them.

Psalms 145:18-19

You are ashamed to come to me when you're feeling so desperate. You're afraid that I will be ashamed of you.[1] You think that you're a bad Christian when you feel so desolate.

Dear one, you do well to cry out to me. I'm proud of you! It is my nature to save my children from their enemies. When you call out to me you demonstrate your understanding of my nature.

My ears are attentive to those who call on me in truth.[2] I hold the crushed and brokenhearted close to me.[3] I answer and save those who desire my wisdom and hunger after purity and virtue.

It pleases me that you are not like those who call upon me with fraudulent fervency. Their desperation creates such a deafening roar; their bleating and much weeping drown out the sound of my voice. They call out only for relief from their pain, without a heartfelt desire for truth, wisdom, and the ability to change. They do not view me with reverence and awe. They see me only as a Band-Aid dispenser.

I know how easy it is for you to tell yourself you have no right to ask for my help until you have first made every effort of your own. But, my dear child, you don't need to be perfect before you call on me. I have already provided the Perfect One so that you may call my name with confidence. Your perfection, outside of Christ, is neither required nor possible. Your attitude is more important to me than your "footwork." Those who call on me in truth are those who are humble and willing to change;[4] those whose cries are an invitation to me to transform them and deliver them from all their trouble.[5]

I fulfill the desires of those who demonstrate reverence and awe toward me. Call upon me and I will hear your cry and I will heal you. I will save so that you are truly safe.[6]

[1]Psalms 31; [2]Psalms 34:15; [3]Psalms 34:18; [4]Psalms 18:27; [5]Psalms 41; [6]Jeremiah 17:14

74 ~ When Your Faith Is Weak

A bruised reed he will not break, and a smoldering wick he will not snuff out.

Isaiah 41:26

Go gently my child,
    your faith is nearly spent.
You are as fragile and brittle as a bruised reed.
You feel as though a careless move
    or a stiff wind
    could break you.
Come here and sit with me awhile.
Let me shelter you from the wind.
Your flame has dwindled to a spark.
A careless breath could snuff it out.
Let *my* breath restore your flame to full strength.[1]
Seek also
    what strength and encouragement
    may be had from the past.
Let me encourage you with tales of others
    whose faith I have renewed.[2]
It's true, I call some to be strong—to perform mighty works in my
    name. I call a few to be Samsons—to slay lions and lay waste the
    temples of idols.[3] But most of my people are not called to
    demonstrate particular strength.
Rather, like you,
    they are called to demonstrate
    my strength in their weakness.[4]
Most are called to be young Davids,
    with more faith than weaponry—
    slaying giants with meager weapons,
    despite themselves and their circumstances,
    not because of them.

Satan calls you to spare yourself this "grief" ... to cut faith short. He whispers in your ear, "See, it's not worth it! Why doesn't God do something?! He's forgotten you. He doesn't care. You're not worth his trouble."

Do not listen to him!

He is a liar and the father of lies.[5]

Listen to me! I will not allow you to be broken; will not allow your flame to be put out. I will shield you. I will shelter you from the wind. I will call you forth in victory.[6]

[1]John 20:22; [2]1 Kings 19:3-18; Matthew 4:1-11; 2 Corinthians 11, 12; [3]Judges 14:6; 16:25-30; [4]2 Corinthians 12:9-10; [5]John 8:44; [6]1 Peter 1:3-9

75 ❧ I Have Overcome the World

... You received the Spirit of sonship. And by him we cry, "Abba, Father."

Romans 8:15

Your mind and heart are so filled with aching there is no room for my comfort. Your cries drown out my voice.
When your heart hurts so much, it is your natural inclination to
    close it up, to protect;
    but
    my precious child,
    how can it be healed that way?
You can close your heart up around your pain, poking at the wound
    with a thousand recountings of it or,
    my lovely one,
    you can trust me.[1]
Turn your face toward me. Gaze into my eyes.
Wash your mind with the refreshing of my Word.
Drink deeply of it. Let your soul feast on it.
Soothe your heart with the balm of my Spirit.
Draw your life—your every breath—from me.[2]

Privately, you suspect me of turning away from you, I know. You would never say so aloud, but I know. When you are in so much pain you equate me with some earthly fathers who abandon their children when they become inconvenient.
My lovely child, this world is filled with troubles.
That's why I sent my Son, so that he could vanquish the troubles of the world on your behalf.[3]
I know, when you hurt so profoundly you don't *feel* as if your troubles have been vanquished.
They seem so ever-present, so overwhelming.
But listen to my still small voice within you. Do you hear it?
It tells you that I hear your cries.

It tells you the glory that awaits you is so much greater than the suffering you know now, there is no comparison.[4]

It tells you that
   I have the power
        to utilize your pain
                to shape you into a more accurate reflection
                  of my Son.[5]
                        I love you *that* much!

Relax in my embrace. Don't be like others who push against me, flailing against my restraints, straining to be their own masters. They are their own worst enemies. They don't even realize how immeasurably they increase their pain, robbing themselves of healing and joy.

Open your heart to me. Cry out to me in your pain,
   "Daddy! God!"
      I am here!

[1]John 14:1; [2]John 15:1-17; [3]John 16:33; [4]Romans 8:18;
[5]2 Corinthians 3:18

76 ✣ When Plagued by Fear

Say to those who are of a fearful-hearted, "Be strong, do not fear! Behold, your God will come... He will come and save you."

Isaiah 35:4, NKJV

Little one, come into my arms and let me comfort you. Let me remind you of who I AM.

I command angels!

And I have assigned them to guard over all who make me their dwelling place. My angels will lift you up in their hands so that you won't even bruise your foot on a stone. When you abide in me you can stroll past the gates of hell without fear![1]

I am just and honorable!

All that my justice demands has been fulfilled through the shed blood of my dear Son. You need not fear punishment. I hold you in the palm of my hand. No injustice can overtake you.[2]

I am powerful!

I stretch out the heavens with my hands to shelter you like a canopy. I splash the hills with sunlight in the morning and dust the night sky with diamonds. I govern the seasons: Buds blossom at my command... leaves turn to flame. I have the power to depose kings and dictators. Entire nations are a drop in the bucket to me.[3]

I am faithful!

You can be sure of my faithfulness. Claim it as your shield and defense. There's no need to fear the terror that lurks in the dark shadows of night. I will strengthen you. I will protect you from the schemes of your Enemy. The only power fear has is the power you give it.[4]

I am LOVE!

How can you know I love you? I sent my one and only Son into the world to die so that you might enjoy life with me eternally.

Surely such a lavish gift tells you something about my love for you. You can rely on my love. It is perfect, eternal, and able to drive away all fear... for there is no fear in love.[5]

I am victorious!

My Son purchased my victory with his blood. You were created and called expressly to share my victory. When Christ Jesus ascended into heaven to be seated on the Throne he guaranteed your participation in my victory. Draw on my strength and courage, my precious child. Don't be afraid. I am with you always.[6]

[1]Psalms 91:9-12; [2]Deuteronomy 32:4; Psalms 25:10; [3]Isaiah 40:15, 23; Daniel 2:21; [4]1 Thessalonians 5:24; Psalms 91:4b-6a; 2 Thessalonians 3:3; [5]1 John 3:1; 4:9, 16, 18; [6]1 John 4:4; Joshua 1:9; Ephesians 4:8

77 ☙ Help in Time of Need

For he will deliver the needy when he cries, the poor also,
and [one] who has no helper.

Psalms 72:12, NKJV

Your cares have bred icy tendrils, inching
    to encircle your heart
    so that you can no longer feel
    my comfort, tenderly offered.
You feel only your great need.
Day and night
    your need echoes in your mind,
    drumming with the cadence of your apprehensive heart.
Cry out to me, my (anxious) cherished one.
Call my name boldly, with shameless expectation.[1]
Those who are utterly dependent on me
    are always close to my heart;
    their needs are continually before me.[2]
You can trust me always.
Pour out your heart to me,
    tell me your need,
    for I will answer.[3]
Ask and keep asking. Do it boldly because you know that I will only
    give you good things,
    never evil.[4]
My help is always at hand
    because, you see, you have received
    my promise of tomorrow, today.

Today, you have a Helper and Comforter—a token of your future inheritance—sealed within you until that day when you will receive your birthright in full.[5] I am the Author of justice.

I will not allow those who intend you harm to escape what they deserve.[6]

Only remember, their unjust actions are under my control. They mean to harm you but I mean *all* your circumstances for your good.[7]

Call my name. Come and worship me. I will see that you dwell in safety. I will hold you up with my strong arms. Only trust in me.[8]

---

[1]Luke 11:1-13; [2]Psalms 9:12; 12:5; [3]Psalms 62:8; [4]Luke 11:9-13; [5]2 Corinthians 1:18-22; 5:1-5; Ephesians 1:11-14; [6]Psalms 9; [7]Genesis 50:20a; [8]Deuteronomy 3:27

78 ✌ Kept in God's Love

Now to him who is able to keep you from stumbling, and to present you faultless before the presence of his glory with exceeding joy, to God our Savior, Who alone is wise, be glory and majesty, dominion and power, both now and forever.

Jude 24-25, NKJV

Do you trust me, little one? Do you believe that I am able to keep you from stumbling?[1] In your striving to do better, to be more, you have lost sight of Who it is that is really doing the work here.[2] I am pleased with your single-minded desire to be all I created you to be, but you will arrive there more quickly if you relax and relinquish the control to me.

I have often wept while you beat yourself up over your mistakes. I would *never* treat you that way. So why do you?

Walking with me brings joy and refreshment.[3]

You will endure trials but, when you trust me, even times of trial will carry a bittersweet joy.

… Joy at being molded into a more beautiful vessel.

You are so busy pushing and pulling, berating, and re-molding yourself that you seldom perceive my joy. Frequently, I must come behind all of your pushing and pulling and repair the hurt you have inflicted upon yourself.

STOP, dear one, and leave the molding to me.

You have forgotten my plan for the division of labor in your life. Let me remind you, molding is part of *my* job description.[4]

Your job is only to be willing and pliable

… willing and pliable.

I have the power to see that you come to my throne, faultless and pure. I chose you. You are my gift to myself and, trust me, when the time comes I will see to it that you are not a misshapen, half-baked vessel. I am able to make you into a consecrated vessel of honor, sprinkled with Christ's blood.[5] When you are presented before my throne, all of heaven will rejoice over the beauty and perfection you reflect.

[1]Ephesians 3:20-21; [2]Ephesians 2:10; [3]Psalms 100; Acts 3:19; [4]Romans 9:16-21; Jeremiah 18:1-10; [5]1 Peter 1:2

79 ᧞ The Peace of God

*The Lord is near. Do not be anxious about anything, but
in everything, by prayer and petition, with thanksgiving,
present your requests to God. And the peace of God, which
transcends all understanding, will guard your hearts
and your minds in Christ Jesus.*

Philippians 4:5b-7

My beloved child, I am right here with you
   —within you—
   always.
My name is Peace.[1]
Let me breathe peace into your spirit;
   there is no need for you to be troubled.[2]
Bring your fears and concerns to me so that I may assure you that I
   am still seated on the throne;
   I still watch over you.
Nothing can happen to you without my knowledge.
Life's events are sometimes difficult, but I am still in control.[3]
Bring your fatigue and failures to me so that I may give you a
   strength that leads to peace.[4]
Lay claim to the righteousness that is yours
   through my son, Jesus Christ.
Genuine peace springs from righteousness[5]
   … and you have already received
   the righteousness of Christ Jesus,
   credited to you on the day you believed.[6]
Ask for anything in his name and I will give it to you.[7]
Allow my Word to wash away every doubt,
   to scrub away every fear
   from your mind.
Reach to me.
My Holy Spirit will give you a love for my Word.
Those who love my Word are at peace,[8]

surefooted on a straight path.[9]

As you drink in my Word it will produce fruit; you will blossom forth with love, joy, and peace.[10]

[1]Judges 6:24; [2]John 14:27; [3]Psalms 11:4 [4]Psalms 29:11; [5]Psalms 85:10; [6]Galatians 3:6-9, 22; [7]John 14:13; 1 John 5:14-15; [8]Psalms 119:165; [9]Proverbs 3:5-6; [10]Galatians 5:22

80 ❧ Nourished by God's Word

Blessed is the [one] who does not walk in the counsel of the wicked.... But [whose] delight is in the law of the Lord, and on his law meditates day and night. [That one] is like a tree planted by streams of water, which yields its fruit in season and whose leaf does not wither.

Psalms 1:1-3

Seek my ways. Thirst for my wisdom.
Pitch your tent in the lush garden of my Word,
   day and night.
Pray for my principles to flow through your veins
   —down to the very depths of your being—
   so that your thirst is quenched.

Those who keep company with the casually irreverent—those who would not think of demonstrating awe in the face of my power and magnificence—will be scattered like dust blowing in the wind when judgment comes.[1]

Those who practice the mental trickery of godless men—those who rationalize and justify their own self-aggrandizing words and actions—will be brought to destruction.

But you, my child... you will flourish.[2]
You will sink your roots deeply
   into the rich soil of my constant provision.
You will be continually refreshed
   by clear, cool, life-giving water
   ceaselessly flowing through your spirit,
   renewing you day by day,
   moment by moment.
Your branches will be laden with fruit, glistening
   with the reflected light of my Son,
   filling the air with a sweet fragrance.[3]

All you do will prosper.[4]
    Cling to me! Take my law seriously!
        I keep close watch
            over those whose lives demonstrate my righteous ways.[5]

[1]Psalms 1:4; [2]Psalms 1:1; [3]Ephesians 5:1-2; Philippians 4:18-20; [4]Psalms 1:3b; [5]Psalms 1:6

81 ✌ When You Need Wisdom

If any of you lacks wisdom, he should ask God, who gives generously to all without finding fault, and it will be given to him.

James 1:5

Because I am a wise God, I am delighted to give you wisdom when you ask. Because I am a compassionate God, I will not use your request for wisdom as an opportunity to remind you of your shortcomings, rather, I will give to you generously, out of my abundance.

But when you ask, ask with an absolute certainty —no doubt at all—that I hear and answer prayer.

The person who prays with doubt in her heart
    has the emotional stability of a styrofoam cup
    being blown by the wind,
    one minute believing and the next,
    crestfallen and absolutely sure
    I will not answer her.[1]
Why put yourself through that?
You believe in me,
    believe also in my ability and willingness
        to answer your prayers.[2]

I *am* able. In fact, I have the power to do far more for you than you will ever think to ask.[3] Trust me to see that you have all that you need—including wisdom—to accomplish everything I ever ask of you.[4]

Cling to me stubbornly because you know that I always help my children. You will not remain perplexed. You will not wander, lost and confused, because I will guide you as you go, I will lead you in paths of righteousness. [5]You will have nothing to be ashamed of.[6]

So wait expectantly for my answer to your prayer for wisdom. Wait with your heart full of hope because I have said that I will answer.[7]

[1]James 1: 6-8; [2]John 15:7; 16:23-24; Matthew 21:22; Mark 11:24; 1 John 3:22; [3]Ephesians 3:20-21; [4]2 Corinthians 9:8; [5]Psalms 32:8; Psalms 23:3; [6]Isaiah 50:7; [7]Psalms 130:5

82 ❧ Unjustly Accused

Though you search for your enemies, you will not find them. Those who wage war against you will be as nothing at all. For I am the Lord, your God, who takes hold of your right hand and says to you, Do not fear; I will help you.

Isaiah 41:12-13

Your heavy heart has not escaped my attention, my cherished one. I know your grief. Let me gently remind you that you are in good company; my Son was unjustly accused also.

I am not oblivious to your pain. I know that times like these are difficult for you, but cling to me and continue to give a soft answer to everyone who accuses you.[1] I will defend you with the power of my virtuous right hand.[2]

Be patient, my lovely child. Do not be tempted to respond to this injustice on your own behalf; I have reserved vengeance for myself alone.[3] In due time I will cover you in the honor of my name, so wait patiently for me to resolve this difficulty.[4] Wait expectantly while I prove to you that I am your help and shield, that your reputation will not be eternally sullied. My love will never fail you.[5]

This injustice doesn't have the power to separate you from my love.[6] You will emerge more than simply victorious, you will emerge proven and matured.[7] Your vindication will spring from behaving in accordance with my Word.

If the one who has wronged you has a need, meet it with a loving, generous heart. In doing so, you will warm him from the top of his head right down to his sightless heart. In that way you will overcome evil with good and perhaps the eyes of your enemy's heart will be enlightened as a result, and your reward will be great.[8]

Above all, my lovely, obedient child, forgive the one who has hurt you. I know that you view such forgiveness as a lofty ideal, not at all practical, but I have commanded forgiveness for your sake, not mine... or your enemy's. Unforgiveness keeps you fastened to your enemy while forgiveness sets you free. Or would you rather be bound to your enemy forever?

Choose to surrender to me. Make the very practical choice to live according to my revealed will. When you forgive others it opens your life's door to blessings beyond measure, not the least of which is my forgiveness for you.[9]

[1]Proverbs 15:1; 25:15; [2]Isaiah 41:10 [3]Deuteronomy 32:34, 35; Romans 12:19; [4]Psalmss 23; 94; 110; [5]Psalms 33:20-22; [6]Romans 8:37-39; [7]Romans 5:1-5; James 1:1-5; [8]Proverbs 25:21, 22; Ephesians 1:18-23; [9]Matthew 6:9-15

83 ✥ Strength for the Weary

Those who hope in the Lord shall renew their strength.
They will soar on wings like eagles; they will run and not
grow weary; they will walk, and not faint.

Isaiah 40:31

You've worked so hard to win this battle. Do you think perhaps
you've lost sight of the source of your strength?

Remember,
    it is my desire and intent
        to fight the battle for you;
            you only need to stand.[1]

You are so terribly weary. Even now your hope is slipping
through listless fingers. Strength seeps from your pores as if your
very cells are too tired to hold themselves erect. Fatigue rests on
your shoulders like a shroud.

Climb into my lap and rest awhile.

Lean your head upon my chest and listen to the way my heart
beats for you.

Feel the warmth of my arms around you.

You can trust me to show you how to follow me. I am not in the
habit of hiding my ways from my children. You need not hack a
way through the underbrush to find my path. Both are laid out
clearly for you in my Word.

You can count on my mercy and love.

I will guide you to my truth and teach it to your heart when you
reach it.[2]

I will never turn my back on you or leave you standing alone in
the midst of battle.[3]

You can safely whisper "hope" to your heart with the regularity of a ticking clock, measuring off the day in

   hope...

          hope...

                 hope...

because I am faithful forever[4]
and my love for those who revere me extends
through the vast reaches of time—
from before the beginning to the end which has no end.[5]
My grace and mercy never dwindle.[6]

Rest in me, and my Holy Spirit will make you overflow with hope, joy, and peace[7] so that your strength through me is renewed as you hope in me.

[1]Ephesians 5:10-18; [2]Psalms 25:4-6; [3]Joshua 1:5; Deuteronomy 31:6; [4]Psalms 146:6; [5]Psalms 103:17-18; [6]Lamentations 3:22; [7]Romans 15:13

84 ॐ Looking for Wisdom

To the one who pleases him, God gives wisdom, knowledge and happiness....

Ecclesiastes 2:26

How delighted I am that you have come to me for wisdom. You demonstrate the wisdom you already possess by coming to the Possessor of all wisdom instead of seeking human answers.

And my wisdom is more precious than rubies.[1]

It was by wisdom that I set the earth on its foundation,
   by understanding I hung the heavens above.
It was by knowledge that I divided the water from the land,
   and gently instructed the dew to take its place beneath the dawn.[2]
The answers you need are not a mystery to me; I am the revealer of
   mysteries.[3] I am the teacher of all wisdom.[4] Truth, knowledge,
   and understanding are the very languages I speak.[5]
What untold pleasure it gives me
   to share my answers and solutions with you.[6]
It is my joy to fill you
   with the knowledge of my will for your life.
It is my delight to give you
   all spiritual wisdom and understanding
   so that you can live a life worthy of me,
   so that you may please me in every possible way.[7]
Tell me about your problem
   —not so that I will know
   (for I already know)—
   but so that you will be discerning.

Describe to me every aspect of the problem with a worshipful attitude, submitting the problem and all of its parts to me. Once you have done that, your mind will be clear and your heart will be ready to receive the solution when I give it to you.[8]

Give your questions and problems to me, asking for my will only,[9] and wait patiently and joyfully for my magnificent solution.[10]

[1]Proverbs 8:11; [2]Proverbs 3:19, 20; Romans 11:33; [3]Daniel 2:47; [4]Psalms 51:6; [5]Proverbs 2:6; 8:7; [6]Ephesians 1:9; [7]Colossians 1:9-10; [8]Acts 4:24-31; [9]Psalms 40:8; 143:10; Romans 12:1-2; [10]Psalms 37:7-9; 40:1-3; Colossians 1:10-12; James 5:10-11

85 ᢌ When You Worry for Your Children

I will give them a heart to know me, that I am the Lord.
They will be my people, and I will be their God, for they
will return to me with all their heart.

Jeremiah 24:7

I am God, the creator of all you see.
I alone am Lord, there are no other gods beside me…
   no other god can satisfy the longing of the human heart.[1]
Rest on my assurance that I hear your prayers for your child;
   you do not seek me in vain.[2]
I am faithful to fulfill my Word.
The constancy of creation
   testifies to my power and faithfulness.[3]
Your child is never far from my sight.
I watch him arise in the morning
   and go to sleep at night.
I fashioned your child's heart
   with the same delicate intricacies and care
   as your own.[4]
I will be as faithful to your child as I have been to you,
   so pray fervently and wait patiently
   until the day you witness my deliverance
   in your child's life.[5]
Then he will return to me with his whole heart
   and acknowledge me as Lord.

I fulfill every oath, every pledge I have made to my chosen ones.[6] My promise to forgive and save is not only to you but to your children also, even those who have strayed far off the path of righteousness.[7]

Every covenant child will return to my side at the appropriate time. Then I will clothe him in the best robes and place a ring on his finger and all the inhabitants of heaven will rejoice at his return.[8]

And he will live in my presence forevermore.[9]

Do not fret and worry because the path I have chosen for your child is different from my path for you.[10] I love your children even more than you do—more than you can possibly imagine.

[1]Isaiah 45:18; [2]Isaiah 45:19; [3]Genesis 1:1-2:3; 9:8-17; Psalms 33:6-12; [4]Psalms 33:13-15; Psalms 139; [5]Psalms 62:8; John 16:24; [6]Psalms 111:4-9; [7]Acts 2:36-39; 16:31; [8]Luke 15; [9]Psalms 102:28; [10]1 Peter 5:7

86 ᔆ In God's Service

A generous man will prosper; he who refreshes others will himself be refreshed.

Proverbs 11:25

Your longing to give of yourself and your resources is a reflection of my character. I made you the loving, giving person that you are. So turn a deaf ear to the voices that assault you from every bustling intersection, that accuse you of "co-dependence" and "victim-thinking." Refuse to feel guilty or unsure when you acknowledge your impulse to give of yourself.

There is a vast difference between serving others for my sake and serving in order to satisfy a need for significance, safety, or love. One is true worship, the other is servitude to the idol of self (masquerading as "co-dependence"). Carefully weigh your motives for serving and do not be tricked into paying homage to self in the guise of service to me. It is easy to tell the difference. If you spend yourself in meeting others' needs for my sake, I will make you shine with a radiance that rivals the sun. I will renew your strength.[1] You will flourish like a fragrant, well-watered garden. When I am your source, your energy will be renewed like a spring whose waters flow from deep within the earth, never drying up.[2] The god of self is a miserly god who can only impart a hermit-soul, pinched by despair and cowering in an empty corner of gloom.

Those who tell you that you must be careful to keep enough for yourself have never feasted on my grace.[3] Those who caution you not to give too much have never gathered from the abundance at the foot of the Cross.[4] Those who remind you to be careful to maintain your dignity have never had their feet washed by the Savior.[5] Whoever warns you not to lose your self robs you of the chance to find Life.[6] The one who shelters in the presence of the god of self, who focuses on her feelings, her needs, her personal goals cannot experience the wonder and liberty of dwelling in the Presence of the Almighty.[7]

When you give, I give more. I pour out blessings on you according to my own standard of measure, pressed down, shaken together, and overflowing.[8]

The worship of self is foolishness; my way is the way of wisdom. I shield those who are wise enough to lead virtuous lives, I protect those who are faithful to fulfill my calling. Victory is the future of the faithful.[9]

When you serve in my name, my love, mercy, and compassion will flow through you so that you will be completely capable and equipped at all times to do the good works I have called you to perform.[10]

[1]Isaiah 40:28-31; Psalms 103:1-5; [2]Isaiah 58:10-11; [3]Psalms 37:4; 107:9; Ephesians 1:18-23; [4]Matthew 5:6; 2 Corinthians 3:5; 9:6-8; Philippians 4:19; [5]John 13:1-17; [6]Matthew 10:39; [7]2 Peter 1:3-4; [8]Ecclesiastes 11:1; Luke 6:38; [9]Proverbs 2:1-15; [10]2 Corinthians 9:8

87 ᗡ Weep No More

*For behold, I create new heavens and a new earth; and
the former shall not be remembered or come to mind.... I
will rejoice... and joy in my people; the voice of weeping
shall no longer be heard....*

Isaiah 65:17-19, NKJV

Come, my precious one, weep no more.
Dwell, instead, on thoughts of eternity.
In the face of such a hope,
    what cause is there for sadness;
    what can possibly compare to paradise?
Come! Bask in the warmth and light of the Son
    in a place that has no night.[1]
Drink freely from a Spring whose source is without end.[2]
Come! Sup with me at my banquet table.
Eat and be satisfied.[3]
Walk with me down the great street
    of the New Jerusalem to the wondrous tree
    spanning the river there.
Relish fruit from the tree of life,
    no longer forbidden.[4]
Feast on its abundant harvests,
    draw healing from its leaves.[5]
Contemplate a place where there will be no tears
    because there will be no reason to weep.
Fatigue and sickness will be unknown.[6]
There will be no broken friendships,
    no loved ones lost to the grave.[7]
There will be no poverty, pain, prejudice, or persecution.
Envision a City of safety
    whose inhabitants will never again
    know fear or sadness.[8]
Make much of your hope in Christ Jesus.

Such a hope will sustain when
    all else crumbles in your hands.

[1]Revelation 21:23, 25; 22:5; [2]Revelation 21:6; [3]Revelation 19:9; [4]Genesis 3:22-24; Revelation 2:7; [5]Revelation 22:2-3 [6]Isaiah 33:24; Revelation 4:8; [7]Revelation 21:4; [8]Revelation 21:27

88 ๛ Acceptable Worship

... *The prayer of the upright is [God's] delight.*
Proverbs 15:8

Your heart aches with a longing to offer true worship to me, the Lord of All. Night and day, each beat of your heart telegraphs its cry toward heaven, "Teach me to praise you, Lord. Teach me what it means to worship you in spirit and truth."[1]

My adoring child, you already know. Your very request— sincerely made—is worship to me.

You worship me every time you savor my creation; each time you revel in the color of the sky or the rustling wind in the trees. When you enjoy the tastes and smells of the food you eat (food I created) you worship me. Your gratitude for such gifts is true worship.[2]

When you ask me to meet your needs you are worshiping me. That surprises you, doesn't it? It's true nonetheless. When you bring your requests to me you are acknowledging my power to answer.[3] You are demonstrating your desire to see my glory increase as I reveal myself—my faithfulness, wisdom, mercy, and compassion. You are declaring before the host of heaven that you trust me, your conviction that I am real. And when you thank me for answering your prayers, your thanksgiving is a fragrant offering of incense.[4]

When you display your faith, trust, and obedience through a repentant heart your spiritual sacrifice is better than all the sacrifices of old put together.[5] When you trust me to forgive, you not only offer spiritual worship, you perform your calling as a holy priest in my living temple.[6]

Giving attention to my Word—whether in private study or corporate teaching—is true worship.[7]

Taking joy in Christian relationships is a thank offering to me for having knit your hearts together, for having called you to be members of the same Body.[8]

Any demonstration of mercy and compassion for one less fortunate than you is a form of spiritual worship that is most precious to me.[9]

When you sing with a heart full of thanksgiving, your offering of praise pleases me.[10]

Even the running conversation you keep with me as you go about your work each day is true worship (although you half suspect you're bothering me).[11]

Do not be troubled anymore, my lovely child. Stop searching high and low for the "proper" way to worship me. My Holy Spirit has already taught you how.[12] Let my peace stand as a sentry at the door to your heart. Your worship delights me. I am with you, now and forever.[13]

[1]John 4:23; [2]Psalms 29; 93; Hebrews 12:28-29; [3]Psalms 141:2; [4]Psalms 50:12-15; [5]1 Samuel 15:22; Psalms 51:15-17; 107:17-22; Romans 12:1-2; [6]1 Peter 2:4-6; [7]Psalms 40:6-10; Hebrews 11:6; [8]Philippians 1:3; 1 Thessalonians 3:6-13; [9]Deuteronomy 10:17-19; Hosea 6:6; Matthew 5:16; Luke 6:35-36; Philippians 4:18; Hebrews 13:15-16; James 1:27; [10]Psalms 69:30-31; [11]Colossians 3:15-17; 1 Thessalonians 5:17; [12]John 14:16-17; 16:13-14; [13]Philippians 4:6-9

89 ᔯ Regretting the Past

To everything there is a season, a time for every purpose under heaven....

Ecclesiastes 3:1, NKJV

Time seems to bear down on you, merciless, inflexible. You feel like the accumulated failures and losses of your life litter your past like so many lumps of coal. You watch, feeling helpless, while each day seems to vanish in the air like smoke.[1]

Your reflections are full of sighing. But you can't stop time or even mold it into a more pleasing shape. Its wrinkles can't be shaken out so that it can be used over again. Time spent recovering from the backwash of others' sins can never be reclaimed. Years lived for self—in the pursuit of career, possessions, and accolades—are gone forever.

But take heart, my love. Your times are in my hands[2] and I am the Redeemer; it is my business—my delight—to redeem.[3] I will redeem all your lost years. I will redeem the years that peril, and anger, and pain, and self-interest have devoured.[4]

I make everything beautiful in its time.[5] I will use the pressure of time to make all your lumps of coal into diamonds.

I am the Wheel within the wheel of time.[6] My purposes continue to progress as unwaveringly as time itself. I selected every aspect of your life—right down to the speed at which your hair grows—before I ever set the earth beneath my canopy of light.[7] My plan to fully redeem has been in place for just as long.

My plan to redeem your past, however, calls for mutual participation. Your most effective tool for redeeming your past is living every moment of the present for me. To live life every moment for my glory requires grace and no imitations will do. Grace gained by earning others' praise is a mirage. Even grace tenderly offered by a nurturing mother is fleeting. Grace extended through teaching and prayer by one of my servants will not provide you with the power to live for me, although such graces can help to infuse you with the desire to perceive and reach for *my* grace.

In the process of redemption, the only intercession that really matters is Jesus Christ's. The only One who can give you the energy, the insight, the willingness... the grace... to live for me is me.

Do not hesitate a moment longer. The words, "Too late," are among the most poignant words one of my children can utter. And cold cinders of regret supply no warmth.

Whatever I do stands forever, unaltered and unalterable, and everything that happens is for one purpose—so that people everywhere will worship me.[8] Inspire them to worship me for the way I have redeemed your past. Live for me now and your regrets will be swept away by the power of my mighty hand.[9]

[1]Psalms 102:1-3; [2]Psalms 31:15; [3]Job 19:25-27; Psalms 34:17-22; 103:1-5; 130; [4]Joel 2:25; [5]Ecclesiastes 3:11; [6]Ezekiel 1:13-21; [7]Acts 15:18; [8]Ecclesiastes 3:14; [9]Psalms 77:15; 118:15; Ephesians 1:15-23; 1 Peter 5:6

90 ‰ We Shall Be Like Him

Now we see but a poor reflection; then we shall see face to face. Now I know in part; then I shall know fully, even as I am fully known.

1 Corinthians 13:12

No one —even with the most fertile imagination—
   has ever envisioned what I have prepared for those who love me.[1]
And no one has *ever* seen me.[2]
Yet the Scriptures provide a window,
   framing me in your view.
Through them you gain the clearest picture,
   despite the fact that the glass is clouded
   by sin and unbelief.
And there is only One whose glass was not cloudy while he walked
   the earth. Sin and unbelief exist in all my other children, regardless of the purity of their faith.[3]
Still, many behold me
   and rejoice for the radiance reflected there,
   even through a misty glass.
And all see more clearly as they are
   progressively sanctified.[4]
Naturally, those who faithfully study my truth and put it into
   practice gain a clearer view of the one who is the Truth.[5]
As you live in purity and ever-increasing holiness you will become
   more and more like my son, Christ Jesus, who is a reflection of
   me.
Right now, you cannot possibly imagine what you will be like
   when he appears in the clouds
   to welcome you on the Last Day.
That has yet to be revealed,
   but be assured,
   you will be changed into his likeness because
   then you will see him clearly, as he truly is.[6]

Do not doubt that I know you better than you know yourself.[7]
And I love you incomparably more than you love yourself.[8]

On that joyous day of Christ's return,
    you will know as you are known,
        you will love as you are loved.

[1]1 Corinthians 2:9-10; [2]John 1:18; [3]Romans 3:23; [4]2 Corinthians 3:18; [5]John 14:6; James 1:23; [6]1 Thessalonians 4:13-17; 1 John 3:2; [7]1 Corinthians 2:10-11; [8]John 3:16

TOPICAL INDEX

SCRIPTURE INDEX